QUIET MOMENTS
WITH GOD

FOR WOMEN

RACINE, WI

Quiet Moments with God for Women
ISBN: 979-8-88898-018-7 - *Paperback*
ISBN: 979-8-88898-019-4 - *Hardcover*
ISBN: 979-8-88898-020-0 - *Ebook*
Copyright © 2022 by Honor Books

Cover design by Faille Schmitz.

INTRODUCTION

Quiet moments — for personal meditation, for fellowship with God — we women need both in order to live balanced lives while meeting the complex demands we face every day.

As our world moves and swirls past us with great speed and intensity, it's tempting to put those quiet times aside and regard them as luxuries rather than necessities. But the truth is — moments of quiet tranquility are critical. They help us define our relationships, our roles, our priorities, and ourselves. Without them, we become slaves to our lifestyles rather than the masters of them.

We hope you will find that the devotionals in this book help you make your quiet moments productive and inspiring. We have selected those that relate specifically to issues women face. And we have made them short enough to fit easily into your special time apart yet long enough to provide a solid kick-off for your day. As you read, we hope that they will draw you closer to God.

STARRY, STARRY NIGHT

Remember when you were a child, lying on your back outdoors, staring up at the celestial stream of stars and moon? All was peaceful and still. How relaxing it was to quietly gaze at the shimmering lights and simply dream! Even as an adult, you are not too old for that. Everyone needs a quiet time to be alone with God, without television, radio, or teaching tapes. If you can't find quiet time, it's because you've given it away. But you can take it back now.

> The heavens declare the glory of God; and the firmament sheweth his handiwork.
>
> PSALM 19:1 KJV

God created you more special than all other things, even the stars in the heavens. The psalmist wrote in Psalms 8:3-5 KJV, "When I consider thy heavens, the work of thy fingers, the moon and the stars, which thou hast ordained; What is man, that thou art mindful of him? and the son of man that thou visitest him? For thou hast made him a little lower than the angels, and hast crowned him with glory and honor."

God has a special place in His heart just for you and wants you to know Him in a more intimate way. The Lord desires this relationship even more than you do. Having your friendship pleases Him.

Don't listen to the lies of the enemy, who tells you that God is angry because you haven't read your Bible lately. As you spend time with God, you will be strengthened. This strength will keep you from throwing in the towel when times get tough. Make your quiet time top priority. Consider it an appointment with God. Mark on your calendar now the time you plan to spend with God each day and give it first place.

So necessary is our friendship to God that he approaches us and asks us to be his friends.

MEISTER ECKHART

I CAN SEE CLEARLY NOW

Between Macon and Valdosta, Georgia, lies a stretch of Interstate 75, known for heavy fog that causes massive pileups of cars, vans, trucks, and campers. Several times each year horrible accidents happen as drivers enter the thick fog. Many can't even see the front of their own vehicles, much less beyond.

The result is a disaster waiting to happen—and often it does. Many people are injured, vehicles are destroyed, and motorists are delayed for hours. The costs to personal property, the city, and the state, as well as the increase in insurance rates are astronomical. But the worst tragedy is the loss of human life.

Drivers involved in these accidents will tell you the same story. They saw the fog but didn't think it was as thick as it turned out to be. They hoped to pass through it safely by turning their blinkers on and driving slowly. These drivers had no idea that many vehicles in front of them had already been forced to stop—often victims of whatever tragedy had occurred to a car or truck ahead of them.

In this life, we may see things through a fog of confusion or circumstances. But the day will come when we can stand before Christ, when we will see Him clearly just as He is, in all His glory. Nothing will be able to cloud the true and living Christ from our vision when we go to Heaven.

The good news is that we don't have to wait. Today, right now, we can see Him clearly through His Word and in the lives of our Godly brothers and sisters.

———————

Heaven is the place where questions and
answers become one.

ELIE WIESEL

DOWNHILL FROM HERE

J ean-Claude Killy, the French ski champion, did more than just work hard at his sport.

When he made his nation's ski team in the early 1960s, he was determined to be the best. He decided vigorous training was the key. Up at dawn each day, he ran up mountains with his skis on—a very painful activity. He endured intense weight training and sprinting because he was determined to do whatever it took to reach peak physical condition.

However, other team members were working just as hard, and in the end it was a change in style, not conditioning, that set Killy apart.

The goal in ski racing is to ski down a prescribed mountain course faster than anyone else. Killy began experimenting to see if he could pare any seconds off his time. He found that if he skied with his legs apart, he had better balance. He also found that if he sat back on his skis when executing a turn, instead of leaning forward as was customary, he had better control, which also resulted in faster times. Rather than regarding his ski poles as an accessory for balance, Killy tried using them to

> Ye are a chosen generation, a royal priesthood, a holy nation, a peculiar people; that ye should shew forth the praises of him who hath called you out of darkness into marvelous light.
>
> 1 PETER 2:9 KJV

propel himself forward.

Killy's style was unorthodox. But when he won most of the major ski events in 1966 and 1967, including three gold medals at the Winter Olympics, skiers around the world took notice. Today, the Killy style is the norm among downhill and slalom racers. Any other "style" would be considered odd.[1]

As Christians we are not called to conform to the world's standards, but to God's standards. Our lifestyle should challenge people to come to Jesus Christ and live according to His higher ways and purposes. The Christian "style" may seem odd to the unbeliever, but in the end, it is the style that will prevail!

Don't be afraid to be a little "unusual" today in the eyes of those who observe you. Your example may help win them over to a championship lifestyle.

If you want to be original, just try being yourself, because God has never made two people exactly alike.

BERNARD MELTZER

PREPARE TO DARE

T rying something new can be frightening, and may even be dangerous. That's why it's much smarter to take a calculated risk than a reckless plunge.

> Every prudent man acts out of knowledge, but a fool exposes his folly.
>
> PROVERBS 13:16

A calculated risk is what Charles Lindbergh took when he decided to fly across the Atlantic, alone, in a single-engine plane. Was Lindbergh fearful? He certainly might have been if he had never flown before, or if he had known nothing about planes. If he hadn't trusted the builder of his plane or his mechanics, he also would have had a good reason to be anxious. And if he had decided to make the trip on a whim, without advance planning, he certainly would have been labeled foolish.

But none of those factors were true in Lindbergh's case. He was an experienced pilot and mechanic who personally spent months overseeing the construction of his plane. He participated in the planning of every detail of his historic flight. The end result was a safe trip, finished ahead of schedule with fuel to spare.[2]

To a great extent, "Lucky Lindy" made his own luck.

Likewise, heroic spiritual moments are nearly always grounded in advance preparation. Moses grew up in Pharaoh's court, unknowingly being prepared for the day he would demand that Pharaoh let his people leave

Egypt. Daniel was a man of prayer years before the king issued a decree banning prayer. The violation landed Daniel in a lion's den, where his prayers of protection were answered.

David was part of Saul's royal court and married to Saul's daughter. This was part of his preparation for assuming the throne one day. The years he spent in the wilderness prepared him spiritually to trust God, and God alone, to preserve him, protect him, and help him rule an empire. Esther prepared herself for a year before she won the "contest" to be queen. She prepared herself again before boldly coming to the king to expose the enemy of her people.

You may not see clearly what God's purpose is for your life, but you can trust in the fact that He is preparing you for it. He will not waste a moment of your life. So make every relationship and experience count today because He is grooming you for future greatness!

I would rather walk with God in the dark
than go alone in the light.

MARY GARDINER BRAINARD

AT LAST . . .

The story is told of a diamond prospector in Venezuela named Rafael Solano. He was one of many impoverished natives and fortune seekers who came to sift through the rocks of a dried-up riverbed reputed to have diamonds. No one, however, had had any luck for some time in finding any diamonds in the sand and pebbles. One by one, those who came left the site — their dreams shattered, and their bodies drained.

> I will praise you, for you have answered me, and have become my salvation.
>
> PSALM 118:21
> NKJV

Discouraged and exhausted, Solano had just about decided it was time for him to give up too. He had nothing to show for months of hard work.

Then Solano stooped down one last time and scooped up a handful of pebbles, if only so he could say he had personally inspected every pebble in his claim. From the pebbles in his hand, he pulled out one that seemed a little different. He weighed it in his other hand. It seemed heavy. He measured it and weighed it on a scale. Could it be?

Sure enough, Solano had found a diamond in the rough! New York jewelry dealer Harry Winston paid Solano $200,000 for that stone. When it was cut and polished, it became known as the Liberator, and it is considered the largest and purest unmined diamond in the world.

You may have been plugging away at a project for weeks, even months or years, without seeing much progress. Today may be the day. Don't give up!

The Scriptures are filled with examples of men and women who, on the verge of disaster or failure, experienced God's creative work in their lives. Remind yourself . . .

- God's Word is true.
- God can part the sea.
- God can heal the incurable.
- God can provide water from a rock and manna from the heavens.
- God can conquer your enemies.
- God can still deliver from the fiery furnace and the lion's den.

Persevere in what He has asked you to do today because your rewards will be greater than you can think or imagine!

Perseverance is the rope that ties the soul
to the doorpost of heaven.

FRANCES J. ROBERTS

SERENDIPITY MOMENTS

Serendipity, according to Merriam-Webster's Collegiate Dictionary, is "the faculty or phenomenon of finding valuable or agreeable things not sought for." We sometimes call it an "accident, dumb luck, or fate," but serendipity has given us new products and better ways of doing things.

We all know examples of serendipity, such as Columbus's discovery of America while searching for a route to India. Maple syrup was discovered by Native Americans when, needing water, they tapped a maple tree and made the first maple syrup as they boiled off the sap. Westward-traveling pioneers looking for water stopped at a stream for a drink and found gold nuggets in it.

> We are his workmanship, created in Christ Jesus unto good works.
>
> EPHESIANS 2:10 KJV

While George Balias was driving his car through a car wash, he had a moment of serendipity that made him a millionaire. As he watched the strings of the brushes cleaning his car, he turned his mind to his list of things to do, among them edging his lawn.

Suddenly an idea "popped" into his head. He took another long look at the strings on the rotating brush. The strings straightened out when turning at high speed but were still flexible enough to reach into every nook and cranny of his car to get it clean. He asked himself,

Why not use a nylon cord, whirling at high speed, to trim the grass and weeds around the trees and the house? His idea—his serendipity—led to the invention of the Weedeater.

Where do we get new ideas? God is the Master behind serendipity! He may not always give you a million-dollar idea, but He will make you more creative. One expert gives this advice: Capture the ideas, jot them down quickly before they are gone, and evaluate them later. Take time to daydream with the Lord. Seek new challenges. Expand your perspective. Learn and do new things.[3]

Remember today that God is your Creator—and the Creator of everything in the universe. Ask Him to inspire you with new ideas that can glorify Him and benefit others. We are co-creators with Him!

Whatever is worth doing at all is worth doing well.

LORD CHESTERFIELD

TAKE A BREATHER

T he fast-paced, relentless duties of life often cause us to declare with a sigh, "I need a breather." We may be voicing more truth than we realize! Medical researchers have discovered that for virtually every person who works—whether at physically demanding manual labor or intellectually demanding white-collar labor—performance level improves when a person breathes properly.

> The Lord God formed man of the dust of the ground, and breathed into his nostrils the breath of life.
>
> GENESIS 2:7 NKJV

Good breathing is defined as regular, deep, and slow. The opposite—uneven, shallow, and rapid—is a sure sign to most physicians that something is seriously wrong. Good breathing is essential for good health. It supplies oxygen to the bloodstream, which is vital for the functioning of all bodily organs, especially the heart and brain.

The Scriptures tell us God breathes His life into us both physically and spiritually. Jesus breathed upon His disciples to impart the Holy Spirit to them. (See John 20:22.) The early church experienced the Holy Spirit as a rushing mighty wind—a manifestation of the breath of God. (See Acts 2:1-2.)

Today in our personal lives, an awareness of the Spirit of God working in us is often experienced as a fresh breeze, one that cleanses and revives us in every part of our being. The word inspiration literally means to have the things of the Spirit put into us.

We do well to take a periodic "breather" in the Lord's presence. When we do, we find the rhythm of our life evens out. We find our spirits are refreshed and renewed at a level deeper than the superficiality of our daily routine.

Pause to receive from the Lord, and see if you don't find yourself slowing down and releasing the tensions of fear, frustration, and futility. You will be able to think more clearly, God's love will flow more freely, and creative ideas will begin to fill your mind.

Take a breather! Inhale deeply of His goodness, strength, and love.

Rest is the sweet sauce of labor.

PLUTARCH

EDITING YOUR LIFE

Disney films are known the world over as the best in animation, but the studio didn't earn that reputation easily. One of the reasons for the level of excellence achieved was the filmmaker himself. Walt Disney was ruthless about cutting anything that got in the way of the unfolding story.

> Seeing we also are compassed about with so great a cloud of witnesses, let us lay aside every weight, and the sin which doth so easily beset us.
>
> HEBREWS 12:1 KJV

Ward Kimball, one of the animators for Snow White, recalls working 240 days on a four-minute sequence. In this scene, the dwarfs made soup for Snow White, almost destroying the kitchen in the process. Disney thought it was funny, but he decided that it interrupted the flow of the picture, so it was edited out.

Often we find ourselves doing "good" things, which are not only unnecessary, but also a distraction from the unfolding story of our lives. Like the soup scene, many of these things are worthwhile or entertaining, but they lack the essential element of being the best use of the time and talents God has given us.

The next time you're asked to take on another "good scene," ask yourself the following questions:

• Does this fit in with the plan God has set before

me — do I have a lasting inner peace about it?

• Will this task help me or others grow closer to the Lord?

• Can I do this without taking away from the time I've already committed to my family, church, job, or friends?

As you pause to consider the rest of today, consider this: When the film of your life is shown, will it be as great as it might have been? A lot will depend on the multitude of good things you edit out of your life in favor of the great things God wants to do through you!

The wisest thing is time, for it brings
everything to light.

THALES

FAULTY ASSUMPTIONS

A traveler at an airport went to a lounge and bought a small package of cookies to eat while reading a newspaper. Gradually, she became aware of a rustling noise. Looking from behind her paper, she was flabbergasted to see a neatly dressed man helping himself to her cookies. Not wanting to make a scene, she leaned over and took a cookie herself.

A minute or two passed, and then she heard more rustling. He was helping himself to another cookie! By this time, they had come to the end of the package. She was angry but didn't dare allow herself to say anything. Then, as if to add insult to injury, the man broke the remaining cookie in two, pushed half across to her, ate the other half, and left.

Still fuming later when her flight was announced, the woman opened her handbag to get her ticket. To her shock and embarrassment, there was her pack of un-opened cookies!

It's so easy to make assumptions about what is happening around us. We expect things to be a certain way based on past experiences and what we already know or

The pride of thine heart hath deceived thee, thou that dwellest in the clefts of the rock, whose habitation is high; that saith in his heart, who shall bring me down to the ground?

OBADIAH 1:3 KJV

have been told about a situation. Assumptions are not always wrong, but they are never to be trusted. Too many times they lead to embarrassment and even destruction.

The Bible tells us that assumption is based on human reasoning and that the driving force behind it is pride. As the verse above says, it is pride—we think we know everything—which allows us to be deceived.

Pride caused the woman in this story to assume she was right and the gentleman was wrong. Instead of seeing him through God's eyes and praying for wisdom to handle the situation, she ignored the man. She was completely blind to his kindness toward her.

When you find yourself in a conflict with others, avoid prideful assumptions by walking in God's love. See other people and situations through His eyes. After all, your vision is limited, but He knows exactly what's going on!

Pride is spiritual cancer; it eats the very possibility of love, or contentment, or even common sense.

C. S. LEWIS

THE GUIDE

Foreigners who wish to explore the wilderness areas of South America alone must be well prepared to face a number of challenges. Those venturing into the Amazon jungles or Andes Mountains without a guide or adequate preparation will quickly find their lives in peril.

In *A Slow and Certain Light*, missionary Elisabeth Elliot tells of two adventurers who stopped by to see her at her mission station. Loaded heavily with equipment for the rain forest, they sought no advice. They merely asked her to teach them a few phrases of the language so they might converse a bit with the Indians.

Amazed at their temerity, she saw a parallel between these travelers and Christians. She writes: "Sometimes we come to God as the two adventurers came to me—confident and, we think, well-informed and well-equipped. But has it occurred to us that with all our accumulation of stuff, something is missing?"

She suggests that we often ask God for far too little. "We know what we need—a yes or no answer, please, to a simple question. Or perhaps a road sign. Something

The Lord shall guide thee continually, and satisfy thy soul in drought, and make fat thy bones: and thou shalt be like a watered garden, and like a spring of water, whose waters fail not.

ISAIAH 58:11 KJV

quick and easy to point the way. What we really ought to have is the Guide Himself. Maps, road signs, a few useful phrases are good things, but infinitely better is Someone who has been there before and knows the way." [4]

In the midst of your busy and stressful day, you may face unexpected situations. Trust God to be your Guide and pray, "Lord, I know this didn't take you by surprise! You knew it was coming and have already made a way for me. I thank You now that You are taking me where I need to go and giving me everything I need to get over the rough spots along the way."

Relying on God has to begin all over
again every day as if nothing had yet
been done.

C. S. LEWIS

A LEATHER-BOUND COVER

D odie Gadient, a schoolteacher for thirteen years, decided to travel across America and see the sights she had taught about. Traveling alone in a truck with her camper in tow, she launched out. One afternoon in California's rush-hour traffic, the water pump on her truck blew. She was tired, exasperated, and scared that in spite of the traffic jam she caused, no one seemed interested in helping.

> Man looketh on the outward appearance, but the Lord looketh on the heart.
>
> 1 SAMUEL 16:7 KJV

Leaning up against the trailer, she finally prayed, "Please God, send me an angel . . . preferably one with mechanical experience." Within four minutes, a huge Harley drove up, ridden by an enormous man sporting long hair, a beard, and tattooed arms. With an incredible air of confidence, he jumped off and went to work on the truck. A little while later, he flagged down a larger truck, attached a tow chain to the frame of the disabled truck, and whisked the whole fifty-six-foot rig off the freeway onto a side street, where he calmly continued to work on the water pump.

The intimidated schoolteacher was too dumbfounded to talk—especially when she read the paralyzing words on the back of his leather jacket: "Hell's Angels—California." As he finished the task, she finally got up the courage to say, "Thanks so much" and to carry on a brief conversation.

Noticing her surprise at the whole ordeal, he looked her straight in the eye and mumbled, "Don't judge a book by its cover. You may not know who you're talking to." With that he smiled, closed the hood of the truck, and straddled his Harley. With a wave, he was gone as fast as he had appeared.[5]

God has a way of opening our eyes, expanding our perspective, and showing us His greatest treasures — people — if we will look beyond our prejudices and preconceived notions. Be open to Him showing you a few of His treasures today!

Don't judge any man until you have walked two moons in his moccasins.

INDIAN PROVERB

ACCEPTING SUBSTITUTES

A recently married woman moved to a small town in Wyoming. Clothing stores were in short supply, and her busy ranch life left little time for the long trips to larger cities to shop. Her situation was made more difficult by the fact that she was a hard-to-fit size. To solve her problem, she began relying on a major store catalog, which carried her size. The printed order forms sent by the store had this sentence at the bottom: "If we do not have the article you ordered in stock, may we substitute?"

> Unto him that is able to do exceeding abundantly above all that we ask or thing.
> According to the power that worketh in us.
>
> EPHESIANS 3:20
> KJV

Since she rarely ordered unless she really needed the article in question, she was hesitant to trust strangers to make an appropriate substitution, but she replied yes, hoping it wouldn't be necessary.

This approach worked well until one day she opened a package from the company and found a letter which read, in part, "We are sorry that the article you ordered is out of stock, but we have substituted . . ." When she unwrapped the merchandise, she found an article of greater quality worth double the price she paid!

On each order after that, the woman wrote "YES" in large red letters at the bottom of the order form by the substitution question. She had confidence the store would provide her with the best they had to fill her order.

When we pray to God, we are wise to add to our requests that we are quite willing to accept a substitution for what we think we need. We can trust God to send us the perfect answer because, as our Maker, He knows what will fit us better than we do. Because He knows the future in a way that we do not, He can answer in a way that goes beyond our highest expectations. Every time He sends "substitutes," we can be sure He is sending something much better than we could have ever imagined.

When life isn't the way you like, like it the way it is.

JEWISH PROVERB

PRAISE BREAK

Rather than take a coffee break today, take a praise break! Take a pause in your day to acknowledge all the specific ways in which the Lord has been good to you. Thank Him for what He is doing in your life, right now, where you are.

> Oh, give thanks to the Lord, for he is good; his lovingkindness continues forever.
>
> PSALM 136:1 TLB

Nothing is too large or too small to be worthy of your praise. Every good thing you have and experience in life ultimately comes from the Lord. Sometimes blessings come directly and sometimes through the talents or skills of others who are inspired or empowered by Him. Give praise for the things you see at hand!

Your praise list may include the following:

- Vacuum cleaners
- Microwave ovens
- Walking shoes
- Budding trees
- Ready access to vital data
- Computer repair people
- An unfailing copy machine

- The postal worker being five minutes late, which gave you time to find a stamp
- A cordial interview
- Willing colleagues
- Doormats and children who remember to use them
- A cake that survived a slammed back door
- A completed phone call
- Spell-check
- Good health
- Fulfilling work
- A loving family and circle of friends

Look around, look down, and look up. You'll never run out of things to be thankful for!

Remember the day's blessings; forget the day's troubles.

PROVERB

TAKE COVER

B ouncing back from disappointment, loss, or an irritating situation can take time. When you're hurting, the thing you need to do is nurse your wounds for a little while, regroup, then go back out and face the world.

> He will cover you with his pinions, and under his wings you may seek refuge; his faithfulness is a shield and bulwark.
>
> PSALM 91:4
> NASB

Wouldn't it be nice if that saying we learned as children were true in our lives today—"I'm rubber; you're glue. Everything you say bounces off me and sticks to you"? What a relief it would be if angry words, dirty looks, and cruel actions had no power to hurt us.

Many of us have frying pans coated with Teflon because food doesn't stick to it. The scientists at Dow Chemical have come up with what might be called the next generation of Teflon: a fluorocarbon formula that can be sprayed or brushed onto a surface. It's been suggested it might be used to repel graffiti on subway walls, barnacles on ships, dirt on wallpaper, and ice on aircraft. This substance is actually an adhesive and an adhesive. Its "base" sticks to whatever it's applied to, but its "surface" repels moisture.

This is a little like being in the world, but not of it. "I pray not that thou shouldest take them out of the world, but that thou shouldest keep them from the evil," Jesus prayed for His disciples in John 17:15 KJV. "As thou has sent me into the world, even so have I also sent them into the world" (v. 18).

We have to come into contact with a lot of negatives throughout our lives, but we don't have to absorb them or let them become part of us. With the help of the Holy Spirit, we can stick to God. Then His presence and power in our lives will not allow us to be coated with anything that will drag us down.

Kind words don't wear out the tongue.

DANISH PROVERB

WHAT A FRIEND!

What a Friend we have in Jesus,

All our sins and griefs to bear!

What a privilege to carry

Everything to God in prayer!

O what peace we often forfeit!

O what needless pain we bear!

All because we do not carry

Everything to God in prayer.

Joseph Scriven, the writer of the hymn "What a Friend We Have in Jesus," had a life of great sorrow. A day or two before their wedding, his fiancee drowned. This tragedy put him in a melancholy state that stayed with him the rest of his life.

> "I have called you friends."
>
> JOHN 15:15 RSV

In spite of his despondent temperament, the power and presence of God were evident in Scriven's life. He was a philanthropist and a devout Christian. He had a reputation as a man "who saws wood for poor widows and sick people who are unable to pay." To other people he was the friend that they had found in Jesus.

Scriven wrote this hymn to comfort his mother in a time of sorrow. He never intended that anyone else would see it, but the manuscript was discovered by a neighbor. When asked if he had written it, Scriven said, "The Lord and I did it between us."[6]

Spend your break today with your Best Friend, Jesus. He didn't die for you so you could go through struggles alone and carry heavy burdens by yourself. He gave Himself so you and He could become friends, and friends always stand by and help each other.

You only need to share your need with the Lord Jesus in prayer to find comfort!

The dearest friend on Earth is a mere
shadow compared with Jesus Christ.

OSWALD CHAMBERS

SUCH AS I HAVE, I GIVE

> Stir up the gift of God which is in you.
>
> 2 TIMOTHY 1:6
> NKJV

The word talent usually evokes images of great musicians, actors, and artists. When we think of talent in this limited sense, however, we feel untalented if we aren't gifted in any of these areas. The truth is, talents come in as many shapes and sizes as there are people, and God has given talent to each one of us.

What are some of the "not-so-obvious" talents? Compassion is one. Do you feel kindness toward someone in a distressing situation? Then you have been given a talent! Use that feeling to write a letter of encouragement to someone you know who is in need. Do you like to plan surprises for people who may otherwise feel forgotten or left out? Then you are gifted! Don't bury that talent—use it instead to bring joy to another person.

Perhaps you have the gift of seeing something good in every individual. That is a gift all Christians need to cultivate. Affirm the good in someone, and then spread the "good news" about them. It usually takes someone else to see and bring out the best in people. You may see a talent in a person he or she doesn't even know about!

Do you have a calm spirit in the midst of calamity? Can you think clearly when surrounded by turmoil? Then you are gifted—and your talent is very much in need. That was a talent Jesus demonstrated when He slept through the storm on a boat, didn't lose sight of His purpose when facing the angry crowd, and faced His death sentence on the cross.

Do you have a cup of cold water to offer another person? Then you have a gift. Use it in the name of Jesus and for the glory of God.

Now think again. What talents do you have?

———————————————

Talent is something God gives you;
experience is something you give
yourself.

DANIEL LOUIS ROTTINGHANS

MOMENTS OF CONTENTMENT

I f anyone knew about "tornado days" — those days when projects and deadlines fly around you in a flurry — it was the apostle Paul. He wrote to the Corinthians that in the course of his life he was beaten to the point of death with whips and rods; stoned and left for dead; shipwrecked; in peril from rivers, bandits, and seas; sleepless and hungry; cold and without adequate clothing; and persecuted virtually everywhere he went. Yet he was able to say to the Philippians, in essence, "I have learned to be in peace, no matter what happens." Paul had learned the key to inner contentment.

> I have learned how to be content (satisfied to the point where I am not disturbed or disquieted) in whatever state I am.
>
> PHILIPPIANS 4:11 AMP

That peace, born of the Spirit in our hearts, is something we should each cherish. When stressful situations attempt to rob us of our peace, we need to ask the Lord to renew His presence within us. This prayer by Louis Bromfield seems to have been written for just those times:

Oh, Lord, I thank you for the privilege and gift of living in a world filled with beauty and excitement and variety.

I thank you for the gift of loving and being loved, for the friendliness and understanding and beauty of the animals on the farm and in the forest and marshes, for the green of the trees, the sound of a waterfall, the darting beauty of the trout in the brook.

I thank you for the delights of music and children, of other men's thoughts and conversation and their books to read by the fireside or in bed with the rain falling on the roof or the snow blowing past outside the window.

You may not be in a place where you have great beauty around you, but you can close your eyes and imagine yourself in such a place. Make that secret chamber of your heart your place of prayer, your place to experience contentment.

The secret of contentment is knowing
how to enjoy what you have.

LIN YUTANG

"FUSSING" WAY TIME

There was a dear old lady from the country who was going on a railway journey for the first time. She was to travel about fifty miles through an interesting and beautiful region and had looked forward to this trip with great pleasure. However, once she boarded the train it took her so long to get her baskets and parcels put away, her seat comfortably arranged, the shades and shutters adjusted, the anxious questions about all the things she had left behind answered, that she was just settling down to enjoy the trip when they called out the name of ENOUGH her station!

"Oh my!" she said, "if I had only known that we would be here so soon, I wouldn't have wasted my time in fussing. I hardly saw the scenery!"

Continuing to "fuss" with things left behind yesterday and things yet to do tomorrow robs us of the joys God brings to us today. If you've said, "I'm too busy to . . several times today, it might be time to review your priorities.

"Do not worry about tomorrow, for tomorrow will worry about itself. Each day has enough trouble of its own."

MATTHEW 6:34

TOO BUSY

Too busy to read the Bible
Too busy to wait and pray!
Too busy to speak out kindly
To someone by the way!
Too busy to care and struggle,
To think of the life to come!
Too busy building mansions,
To plan for the Heavenly Home.
Too busy to help a brother
Who faces the winter blast!
Too busy to share his burden
When self in the balance is cast.
Too busy for all that is holy
On earth beneath the sky
Too busy to serve the Master
But not too busy to die.

UNKNOWN

Contentment comes not from having
more, but from desiring less.

UNKNOWN

SO SEND I YOU

Margaret Clarkson was a twenty-three-year-old school teacher in a gold-mining town in northern Ontario, Canada—far from friends and family. As she meditated on John 20:21 one evening, God spoke to her through the phrase "So send I you." She realized that this lonely area was the place to which "God had sent her." This was her mission field.

As she quickly set down her thoughts in verse, one of the finest and most popular missionary hymns of the twentieth century was born.

Because of a physical disability, Miss Clarkson was unable to fulfill her early desire of going to a foreign mission field. Yet her words have challenged many to respond to God's call for service:

> I heard the voice of the Lord, saying, whom shall I send, and who will go for us? Then said I, here I am; send me.
>
> ISAIAH 6:8 KJV

So send I you to labor unrewarded,
To serve unpaid, unloved, unsought, unknown,
To bear rebuke, to suffer scorn and scoffing —
So send I you to suffer for My sake.

So send I you to bind the bruised and broken,
O'er wand'ring souls to work, to weep, to wake,
To bear the burdens of a world a-weary —
So send I you to suffer for My sake.

So send I you to loneliness and longing,
With heart ahung'ring for the loved and known,
Forsaking home and kindred, friend and dear one —
So send I you to know My love alone.

So send I you to leave your life's ambition,
To die to dear desire, self-will resign,
To labor long and love where men revile you —
So send I you to lose your life in Mine.

So send I you to hearts made hard by hatred,
To eyes made blind because they will not see,
To spend — tho' it be blood — to spend and spare not —
So send I you to taste of Calvary.[7]

"As my Father hath sent me, so send I you" (John 20:21 KJV).

Nothing is impossible to the willing
heart.

THOMAS HEYWOOD

LIVING BEYOND
THE THUNDER

I n *The Diary of a Young Girl*, Anne Frank wrote, "I simply can't build up my hopes on a foundation consisting of confusion, misery, and death."[8] She understood that hope originates somewhere beyond our immediate circumstances. In fact, hope — real hope — often stands alone in the darkness.

> Be strong and take heart, all you who hope in the Lord.
>
> PSALM 31:24

How was this young girl capable of courage and faith far beyond her years? She refused to allow the devastation of her times to shape her view of life. In her words, "It's really a wonder that I haven't dropped all my ideals . . . Yet I keep them. I hear the ever-approaching thunder. I can feel the sufferings of millions and yet, if I look up into the heavens, I think that it will all come right."[9]

We can't know what horrors Anne Frank and her family suffered in the Holocaust, but we do know only her father emerged alive. Yet her words live on. Decades later, several generations have read and been touched by the diary of a young girl facing one of the darkest periods in world history — a girl who chose hope in the midst of hopelessness.

Life sometimes includes hardship. When tests come, we have the same choice Anne Frank had: hold on to our ideals or drop them. When life's circumstances sound like "approaching thunder," remember the simple truth in the life of a young Jewish girl. A foundation made of the right ingredients makes for an overcoming life. Holding tightly to one's ideals no matter the circumstance is a hallmark of character.

In all things God works for the good of those who love him, who have been called according to his purpose.

ROMANS 8:28

THE GOOD LIFE

A popular Internet joke goes something like this:

A secretary, a paralegal, and a partner in a big law firm are walking to lunch when they find an antique oil lamp. They rub it, and a genie comes out in a puff of smoke. The genie says, "I usually only grant three wishes, so I'll give each of you just one."

"Me first!" says the secretary. "I want to be in the Bahamas, driving a speedboat, without a care in the world." Poof! She's gone.

"Me next!" says the paralegal. "I want to be in Hawaii, relaxing on the beach with my personal masseuse, an endless supply of pina coladas, and the love of my life." Poof! He's gone. "You're next," the genie says to the partner.

The partner says, "I want those two back in the office right after lunch."

> The son said unto him, Father, I . . . am no more worthy to be called thy son.
>
> LUKE 15:21 KJV

We've been told for ages that we can "have it all." But there's too much to do, not enough time — and no magic lamp to do it for us. And we wouldn't even want it all if we didn't think it would make us happy.

However, those in the know say there's an easier path to a happy life. These three simple thoughts are cited as the keys to happiness:

1. Fret not—He loves you. (See John 13:1.)
2. Faint not—He holds you. (See Psalm 139:10.)
3. Fret not—He keeps you. (See Psalm 121:5.)

It is possible to have it all . . . by making God your "All."

———————————————

Happiness grows at our own firesides, and
is not to be picked in a stranger's garden.

DOUGLAS JERROLD

MORNING PRAISE!

A young career woman moved away from her home to New York City. She rented a room from an elderly lady who had migrated to the United States years before from Sweden. The landlady offered a clean room, a shared bathroom, and use of the kitchen at a reasonable rate.

The little white-haired Swedish woman made the rules of the house very clear. There would be no smoking or drinking, no food in the bedrooms, etc. Pausing mid-sentence, the landlady asked, "Do you sing? Do you play? Music is good! I used to play the piano at the church, but not now. I'm too old. My hearing isn't good, but I love to praise God with music. God loves music."

> Come before him with joyful singing.
>
> PSALM 100:2
> NASB

Later that evening, after a full day of moving into her new room, the young tenant heard horrible noises coming from somewhere downstairs.

Cautiously making her way down the stairway, she followed the sounds to the kitchen door. There she discovered her new landlady standing at the stove, joyfully "singing" at the top of her lungs!

Never had the young woman heard such a horrible voice. Yet she heard that voice, precious to God, every day for as long as she rented the room just over the kitchen.

The Swedish lady passed into glory a few years later. The tenant moved on, married, and had her own family. She is alone now also, and she has lost some of her hearing. Yet, every morning she stands in front of the stove and sings off key and loud, but joyful, praises to the Lord!

What a glorious way to start the day!

Joy rises in me like a summer's morn.

SAMUEL TAYLOR COLERIDGE

LASTING LEGACIES

Marian Wright Edelman, attorney and founding president of the Children's Defense Fund, often speaks of how Martin Luther King had a profound impact on her life. All Americans have been affected by Dr. King's life in some way, and most have heard his famous comment, "I have a dream." But it was not his public persona that had an impact upon her; it was his willingness to admit his fears.

> Good will come to him who is generous and lends freely, who conducts his affairs with justice.
>
> PSALM 112:5

She writes, "I remember him as someone able to admit how often he was afraid and unsure about his next step . . . It was his human vulnerability and his ability to rise above it that I most remember."

She should know about rising above fear and uncertainty because her life was not an easy one, and one wonders just how often she drew strength from the self-honesty and candor of Dr. King.

Ms. Edelman grew up during the days of segregation, one of five children, the daughter of a Baptist minister. She graduated from Spelman College and Yale University Law School and was the first black woman to pass the bar in the state of Mississippi. She is a prolific and gifted writer and has devoted her life to serving as an activist for disadvantaged Americans, especially children.

Hers is an incredible testimony to the belief in helping others to help themselves. She never doubted that she could make a difference. "I have always believed that I could help change the world because I have been lucky to have adults around me who did—in small and large ways."

We have the same opportunity. Will we respond as well as she? Will we help change the world?

He who gives to me teaches me to give.

DANISH PROVERB

THE INVITATION

R ita stood on the sidewalk, peering wistfully at the beautiful home. Through the curtained windows she saw nicely dressed people chatting with one another and enjoying refreshments. In her hand she clutched an engraved, personal invitation to the dinner party. She had been invited to attend this evening's affair by her professor who was impressed with her academic abilities and wanted her to meet others at the university.

> "The son said unto him, 'Father, I . . . am no more worthy to be called thy son.'"
>
> LUKE 15:21 KJV

She carefully fingered the invitation, looked down at her nice "party dress" that seemed so dull and ordinary in comparison to the gowns she saw through the window, and with a sadness of the soul she turned and slowly walked away. Clutched between her fingers was the unused invitation.

This poignant and painful scene from the British movie Educating Rita demonstrates just how difficult it is for one to accept the possibility of a new life. Rita came from a lower middle class family, and no one had attended university before her. She struggled with feelings of inadequacy and was forever wondering how she would "fit in." It is this sense of self-doubt that caused her to fail to take action on the invitation.

However, thanks to a persistent professor, who saw

more in her than she saw in herself, she eventually accepted his invitation to join a new world. By the movie's end, this once modest woman excels as a scholar.

The invitation to become and then excel as a Christian is for each of us. The greatest joy, though, is in knowing that our Master Teacher always sees much more in us than we usually see in ourselves.

God does not ask about our ability, but our availability.

They can conquer who believe they can.

JOHN DRYDEN

A NEW LOOK

In 1998, twenty-one-year-old Se Ri Pak became the newest "wonder kid" of women's professional golf, winning the United States Open and later becoming the first woman to shoot 61 in an LPGA event. Having played golf for only six years before turning professional, her amazing ascent was attributed not only to talent, but also to a fierce mental focus based in the Asian tradition of controlling one's emotions.

Onlookers are awed at the young player's ability to ignore distractions on the course. Even her caddy was asked if they were fighting because she walks alone and does not talk with him. But he explained that it's because she is intensely focused all the time.

In fact, her control is such that Se Ri broke into tears for the first time in her life upon winning the U.S. Open. Emotional display is that unusual for her. But she explains how she's working to change that habit:

I usually look very serious, but after I started playing golf at fourteen, I saw Nancy Lopez on TV. I didn't know she was a great golfer — all I knew was that she always smiled. My goal is to be that way too. Now when I sign autographs, I always put a smile by my name. . .

. Even if I don't win, I want to give people a smile.[10]

It is said a smile is the best way to improve your appearance. It's also one of the nicest things you can do for others. Pass it on!

_____

A smile costs nothing but creates much.

UNKNOWN

BOOK ME, PAPAW!

His eyes moistened with unbidden tears as Nicole climbed into his lap and settled comfortably against his chest. Her hair, freshly shampooed and dried, smelled of lemons and touched his cheek, soft as down. With clear blue-green eyes, she looked expectantly up at his face, thrust the trusted and well-worn book of children's stories at him, and said, "Book me, Papaw, book me!"

> Children's children are the crown of old men; and the glory of children are their fathers.
>
> PROVERBS 17:6 KJV

"Papaw" James carefully adjusted his reading glasses, cleared his throat, and began the familiar story. She knew the words by heart and excitedly "read" along with him. Every now and then he missed a word, and she politely corrected him, saying, "No, Papaw, that's not what it says. Now let's do it again so that we get it right."

She had no idea how her purity of heart thrilled his soul or how her simple trust in him moved him. James had a far different childhood—one characterized by a harsh existence, made harder still by a distant and demanding father. His father ordered him to work the fields from dawn to dusk beginning in his fifth year of life. His childhood memories sometimes continue to create anger and pain.

This first grandchild, though, has brought joy and light into his life in a way that supersedes his own childhood. He returns her love and faith with a gentleness and devotion that make her world secure and safe beyond measure. Theirs is a relationship made for a lifetime. For Nicole, it lays a foundation for life. For James, it heals a past of pain.

"Book me, Papaw, book me!"

James Dobson sums it up well when he says, "Children are not casual guests in our home."[11]

The world moves forward on the feet of
little children.

HERBERT HOOVER

WITHOUT WORDS

As with many memorials, the Franklin Delano Roosevelt memorial in Washington, D.C., came into being after years of debate. Women's groups demanded that Eleanor be given appropriate recognition. Activists for the disabled ardently believed that FDR should be portrayed in his wheelchair. On and on, the debates raged. Finally, in spite of all the controversy, it was completed.

> Show proper respect to everyone.
>
> 1 PETER 2:17

The memorial gives testimony to the fact that President Roosevelt and his wife Eleanor served America during some of its darkest years. It is a fitting design, for as visitors approach it, nothing really stands out. All one sees is a flat granite wall, perhaps twenty feet in height, with a simple quote from FDR; but this is just the beginning.

The memorial stretches directly away from the entrance. After rounding the wall, visitors move from area to area—every one marked by unique stillness. Each succeeding area is creatively set apart from the previous one, making it a tribute in its own right. Visitors find themselves looking at human-sized sculptures of men and women standing in breadlines, reading quotes decrying the savagery of war, staring eye to eye with Eleanor Roosevelt, and eventually looking up and across to see FDR in his wheelchair with his Scottish terrier beside him.

The strength of the memorial comes from its ability to draw the visitor into the presence of one man's passionate belief in serving his country. The impact of the memorial is that it makes each visitor more aware of the awesome responsibility of leadership—not just the leadership of presidents, but leadership of all people.

Whenever you have doubts about your purpose, remember the words of Martin Luther King Jr., "Everyone can be great because everyone can serve."

A candle loses nothing by lighting
another candle.

PROVERB

FEEL THE POWER!

Pope John XXIII was once quoted as saying, "It often happens that I wake at night and begin to think about a serious problem and decide I must tell the Pope about it. Then I wake up completely and remember that I am the Pope."

Far too often we imagine that the solution to our problems, the cure for our ailments, and the guarantee for our happiness lie with someone or something outside ourselves. But do we really have so little power?

Martha Washington thought otherwise, stating, "I have learned from experience that the greater part of our happiness or misery depends on our dispositions and not on our circumstances. We carry the seeds with us in our minds wherever we go."

Just think about it. How dramatically would your life be changed if you knew you had the seeds to your happiness waiting inside, longing to blossom whenever you would allow it? From the words of Mother Teresa, in her book A Gift to God, we can learn how to let those seeds spring to life:

Whatever is true, whatever is noble, whatever is right, whatever is pure, whatever is lovely, whatever is admirable—if anything is excellent or praiseworthy—think about such things.

PHILIPPIANS 4:8

We all long for Heaven where God is but we have it in our power to be in Heaven with Him right now — to be happy with Him at this very moment. But being happy with Him now means

- loving as He loves,
- helping as He helps,
- giving as He gives,
- serving as He serves,
- rescuing as He rescues,
- being with Him for all the twenty-four hours,
- touching Him in His distressing disguise.

Happiness is not a destination, but a journey.

UNKNOWN

THE FIRST VALENTINE

Most people would be surprised to learn that Valentine's Day was not intended to celebrate romance with gifts of flowers and chocolate. It was a day to honor a different kind of love.

Valentine was a Christian priest near Rome in a period when Christians were punished for rejecting the Roman gods. During this persecution, legends say that Valentine assisted Christians in escaping from prison. He was discovered, arrested, and sent to trial, where he was asked if he believed in the Roman gods. He called their gods false. He continued to say that the only true God was He, whom Jesus called "Father."

> We love, because he first loved us.
>
> 1 JOHN 4:19
> NASB

Valentine was imprisoned, but it did not stop him from continuing his ministry. Even the prison guards began to listen to his witness. One was the adoptive father of a blind girl, whom the priest befriended as she waited at the jail while her father worked.

When the Roman emperor heard of Valentine's persistent worship of his God, he ordered his execution. In the days before his death, Valentine offered to pray for the jailer's blind daughter, and her sight was miraculously restored when he died. As a result, the jailer's entire family — forty-six people — came to believe in the one God and were baptized.

Saint Valentine knew every step of the way that his

activities would endanger his life. But he continued because he loved God and people. It was a love that deserves to be honored and modeled after every day of the year.

Love is like a rose, the joy of all the
Earth.

CHRISTINA ROSSETTI

SAY THAT AGAIN?

I n 1954, Sylvia Wright wrote a column for the Atlantic in which she coined the term monde-green, her code word for misheard lyrics. She wrote about hearing the following Scottish folk song, "The Bonny Earl of Morray":

> Ye highlands, and ye lowlands,
> Oh! whair hae ye been?
> They hae slaine the Earl of Murray,
> And layd him on the green.

She misheard the last line as "and Lady Monde-green." It saddened her immensely that both the Earl and the Lady had died. Of course, she was later chagrined to learn that those were not the lyrics at all. But they made so much sense at the time.

• In "America the Beautiful," one young patriot heard "Oh beautiful, for spacious skies" as "Oh beautiful, for spaceship guys."

So shall my word be that goes forth from my mouth; it shall not return to me void, but it shall accomplish what I please, and it shall prosper in the thing for which I sent it.

ISAIAH 55:11 NKJV

• Another considered "Away in a Manger" a little unsettling as he sang, "The cattle are blowing the baby away."

• Then there was the Mickey Mouse Club fan who, when the cast sang "Forever hold your banners high," thought they were encouraging her to "Forever hold your Pampers high!"[12]

It's no wonder that, with all our earthly static and clamor, we sometimes think we're singing the right words when we're not. But if we begin each day in quiet conversation with God, His Word comes through loud and clear. There can be no misunderstanding God's lyrics.

It takes a great man to make a good
listener.

ARTHUR HELPS

NIGHT DRIVING

A woman confessed to a friend her confusion and hesitance about an important life decision she was facing. She professed to believe in God but could not bring herself to rely on her faith to help choose her path.

"How can I know I'm doing the right thing?" she asked. "How can I possibly believe my decision will be right when I can't even see tomorrow?"

> Thy word is a lamp to my feet, and a light to my path.
>
> PSALM 119:105 NASB

Her friend thought and finally said, "Here's how I look at it. You know when you're driving down a dark country road with no streetlights to give you any notion of where you are? It's a little scary. But you rely on headlights. Now, those headlights may only show you ten yards of road in front of you, but you see where to go for that little stretch. And as you travel that ten-yard stretch of road, the headlights show you ten more yards, and ten more, until eventually you reach your destination safe and sound.

"That's how I feel about living by faith. I may not be able to see tomorrow, next week, or next year, but I know that God will give me the light to find my way when I need it."

When you come to the edge of all the
light you know and are about to step off
into the darkness of the unknown, faith is
knowing one of two things will happen:
there will be something solid to stand on,
or you will be taught to fly.

BARBARA J. WINTER

A WORK IN PROGRESS

Many centuries ago, a young Greek artist named Timanthes studied under a respected tutor. After several years of effort, Timanthes painted an exquisite work of art. Unfortunately, he was so taken with his painting that he spent days gazing at it.

> We are his workmanship, created in Christ Jesus for good works, which God prepared beforehand that we should walk in them.
>
> EPHESIANS 2:10
> NKJV

One morning, he arrived to find his work blotted out with paint. His teacher admitted destroying the painting, saying, "I did it for your own good. That painting was retarding your progress. Start again and see if you can do better." Timanthes took his teacher's advice and produced Sacrifice of Iphigenia, now regarded as one of the finest paintings of antiquity.[13]

Timanthes's teacher knew what many great artists know — we should never consider ourselves truly finished with our work.

When the legendary Pablo Casals reached his ninety-fifth year, a reporter asked, "Mr. Casals, you are ninety-five and the greatest cellist who ever lived. Why do you still practice six hours a day?"

And Casals answered, "Because I think I'm making progress."

Maya Angelou applies that same logic to daily life.

In her book Wouldn't Take Nothin' for My Journey Now, she writes: "Many things continue to amaze me, even well into the sixth decade of my life. I'm startled or taken aback when people walk up to me and tell me they are Christians. My first response is the question 'Already?' It seems to me a lifelong endeavor to try to live the life of a Christian."[14]

How exciting it is to be a work in progress! With God's help, our possibilities are limitless!

No limits but the sky.

MIGUEL DE CERVANTES

FINE CHINA

A ntique hunting one day, a collector noticed a lovely teacup and saucer. The delicate set stood out from the other china pieces in the display. She picked up the cup and examined it carefully. Discovering a small imperfection on the bottom, she lovingly held it in her hands as she thought about what might have caused the cup's flaw.

> Behold, like the clay in the potter's hand, so are you in my hand, O house of Israel.
>
> JEREMIAH 18:6
> NASB

A few years earlier while visiting a pottery shop, she had watched as the potter chose a lump of clay to work and began to punch and slam it over and over again until it was just right. He shaped it, painted it, and fired it into a beautiful piece of earthenware that would be looked upon admiringly and be a serviceable item as well.

The clay, useless in its original form, had become beautiful, strong, and useful in the potter's hands. The woman thought of her own life with all its flaws, yet Jesus was willing to sacrifice himself so that she could have a good life with Him. Many lumpy places had existed in her heart prior to her salvation, but Jesus Christ, the Master Craftsman, began His work of shaping and molding, lovingly concentrating on even the finest details. This human vessel was then made fit for His service as He gently filled it to overflowing with the refining work of the Holy Spirit.

As she stepped up to the counter to purchase the cup and saucer, she whispered a prayer. "Lord, help me to never forget what You saved me from, the price You paid, and the hope I have of one day being in Heaven's display as a fine piece worthy of You."

Grace is the love that gives, that loves the unlovely and the unlovable

OSWALD C. HOFFMANN

MORNING DRIVE

This is the day which the Lord has made; we will rejoice and be glad in it.

PSALM 118:24
NKJV

Judy could take the freeway to work each morning and arrive instantly, nerves revved, almost before she is awake. But to her, freeways are ugly. Instead she takes the scenic route around several local lakes and starts her day with mental pictures of sunrises, flowers, and people in various states of running and walking.

She feels that nature is the attraction—a chance for a city slicker to enjoy a little tranquillity. The slower pace gives her the occasion to see a small troop of deer or watch the ducks and geese depart for the winter and return for their spring nesting activities. She recognizes and studies the walkers and joggers who are out regularly at the crack of dawn.

"I don't know if I have a better workday because I sneak up on the job rather than race to it," she muses. "On some mornings, I don't see one thing that nature has to offer because the day ahead refuses to wait for me to get there, and I spend the entire ride making lists of things to do in my head. But I do know that when I take the time to glance at the roses along the way, I feel more fortified, just like our mothers wanted us to be with a hearty breakfast, mittens, and hats."[15]

Taking a few moments to thank God for the glories

of creation will make any day start on a better note!

Lovely flowers are the smiles of God's
goodness.

SAMUEL WILBERFORCE

BY YOUR FRUIT

With these words, Mother Teresa explained a lifetime of service:

> *I can love only one person at a time. I can feed only one person at a time. Just one, one, one. So you begin . . . I begin. I picked up one person — maybe if I didn't pick up that one person I wouldn't have picked up 42,000.*[16]

When she died, an entire world mourned.

Sometime before her death, a college professor asked his students to name people they considered truly worthy of the title "world leader." Although many different names appeared on the class list, the one name most commonly agreed upon was Mother Teresa.

The students wrote the following statements about her:

> *She transcends normal love.*

Love, joy, peace patience, kindness, goodness, faithfulness, gentleness, and self-control. Against such things there is no law.

GALATIANS 5:22-23

She has a capacity for giving that makes me ashamed of my own self-centered actions.

The most remarkable thing about her is that she never grows tired of her work. She never experiences "burnout" like so many other people. I just hope that I can be as satisfied with my life as she is with hers.

Although none of the students had ever met her, they acknowledged that Mother Teresa had a profound impact on each of their lives. How? By her love. She welcomed the opportunity to fulfill her duties. Can we do any less?

Next time you have a chance to be kind, remember her words: "It is not how much we do but how much love we put in the doing."[17] How exciting it is to know that each of us can put enough love into the doing, if we so decide, to be a "Mother Teresa" for at least one other person!

Who knows what would happen if we would all just begin.

Take away love and our Earth is a tomb.

ROBERT BROWNING

MAY I TAKE
YOUR ORDER?

Sometimes, the only solution for a difficult day is a nice double-dip ice cream cone — that is, if you love ice cream. One fan described a recent trial in ordering her treat at a drive-thru window.

She drove up to the speaker to place her order. This ice cream franchise carried too many flavors to list them all on the menu, so customers had to ask if a special flavor was in stock. The attendant answered: "May I take your order?"

> Then shall ye call upon me, and ye shall go and pray unto me, and I will hearken unto you.
>
> JEREMIAH 29:12
> KJV

"Do you have butter brickle today?" she asked. It was her favorite since childhood, and it was becoming increasingly difficult to find.

"No, I'm sorry . . . can we get you anything else?"

Oh, the frustration of drive-thru communication. "What else do you have?" she asked.

The attendant paused and said, "Well . . . what do you want?"

She couldn't help herself. "I want butter brickle!"

It was useless. But, determined to find that flavor, she drove two miles to the next franchise store. She approached the speaker with optimism. "May I take your order?" he asked.

"Yes, do you have butter brickle today?"

After a long pause, the attendant responded, "Butter brickle what?"

It is so disheartening to feel that no one hears our needs. How fortunate that God not only understands our every desire, but also knows them even before we do. Philippians 4:6 ASV encourages, "In nothing be anxious; but in everything by prayer and supplication with thanksgiving let your requests be made known unto God." In His care we are assured our needs will be supplied.

Those who know when they have enough
are rich.

CHINESE PROVERB

GOT CHANGE?

A lecturer once told this story of a counseling patient who hated her job and thought it was ruining her life. But throughout her therapy, she seemed totally unwilling to improve her situation. When he suggested she hunt for a new job, she complained that there were no decent jobs in her small town.

He asked if she had considered looking for a job in the next town, fifteen miles away. She said that she would need a car to travel that far, and she didn't have one. When the therapist offered a plan to purchase an inexpensive car, she countered that it would never work because there's no place to park in the neighboring town anyway!

> God has not given us a spirit of fear, but of power and of love and of a sound mind.
>
> 2 TIMOTHY 1:7 NKJV

It's said that three things in life are certain: death, taxes, and change. If you look around, you'll notice that most people can deal with the first two better than change. But without it, we'll never know how wonderful the plans God has for us can be.

Fear of change comes from fear of loss, even if we are losing something that we never liked in the first place. If you are struggling with change in your life today, take a moment to bring your fears to the Lord. With faith in His guidance, change can lead to a blessing!

Our real blessings often appear to us in
the shapes of pains, losses, and
disappointments; but let us have patience,
and we soon shall see them in their
proper figures.

JOSEPH ADDISON

FAITH IS A VERB

I n *You Can't Afford the Luxury of a Negative Thought*, John Roger and Peter McWilliams offered a new description of faith. They chose the word *faithing* to describe their proactive approach to confidence in life's outcomes.

In their thinking, faithing works in the present, acknowledging that there is a purpose to everything and life is unfolding exactly as it should. It is actively trusting that God can handle our troubles and needs better than we can. All we must do is let them go so that He can do His work.

"THE TWO BOXES"

I have in my hands two boxes
Which God gave me to hold.
He said, "Put all your sorrows in the black,
And all your joys in the gold."
I heeded His words, and in the two boxes
Both my joys and sorrows I store,
But though the gold became heavier each day
The black was as light as before.
With curiosity, I opened the black.
I wanted to find out why.
And I saw, in the base of the box, a hole

80

Which my sorrows had fallen out by.
I showed the hole to God, and mused aloud,
"I wonder where all my sorrows could be."
He smiled a gentle smile at me.
"My child, they're all here, with Me."
I asked, "God, why give me the boxes,
Why the gold, and the black with the hole?"
"My child, the gold is to count your blessings,
the black is for you to let go."[18]

Trust involves letting go and knowing
God will catch you.

JAMES C. DOBSON

SEEING WITH THE HEART

Maria was a kindhearted teacher's aide who simply wanted to "love the children better" in this class for emotionally disturbed students. She could tolerate much, but Danny was wearing her patience out. It had been easier to love him before, when he would try to hurt himself rather than others. And, although Danny was only seven years old, it really hurt when he would hit her.

For many months Danny would withdraw into a private world and try to hit his head against a wall anytime he got upset. But now, he was making "progress" because instead of withdrawing, he was striking out at Maria.

> Give your servant a discerning heart.
>
> 1 KINGS 3:9

"Progress?" exclaimed Maria. "How is it progress for him to want to hurt me?"

"Danny was repeatedly abused as a small child," explained the school psychologist. "He has known only adults who were mean to him or simply ignored his most basic needs. He has had no one he could trust. No one to hold him close; no one to dry his tears when he cried or fix him food when he was hungry. He has been punished for no reason. He's making progress because for the first time in his life, he trusts an adult enough to act out his anger rather than self-destruct. You are that trustworthy adult, Maria."

Upon hearing this explanation, Maria, with tears

spilling from her eyes, exclaimed, "I see!" As comprehension, her anger quickly melted.

John Ruskin wrote, "When love and skill work together, expect a masterpiece."[19]

Sometimes progress seems elusive, but God is faithful to continue the good work He has started in each of our lives. If we will open the eyes of our hearts, we will see His hand at work in our midst.

Do what you can, with what you have,

where you are.

THEODORE ROOSEVELT

PERFECT HARMONY

The late Leonard Bernstein—conductor, composer, teacher, and advocate—may well be the most important figure in American music of the twentieth century. With his personality and passion for his favorite subject, he inspired generations of new musicians and taught thousands that music should be an integral part of everyone's life.

> Do not forsake your friend.
>
> PROVERBS 27:10

As a public figure, Bernstein was larger than life—his charm and persuasiveness infectious. While his career progressed, he was constantly sought after for performances, lectures, and other appearances.

But it's said that in his later years, one way his personal life eroded was in his friendships. There came a time when he had few close friends. After his death, a comment from one of his longest acquaintances was that "you wanted to be his friend, but so many other people sought his attention that, eventually, the friendliest thing you could do was leave him alone."[20]

Scientific evidence now shows us how important friendships are, not only to our emotional health, but to our physical and mental health as well. But these most cherished relationships are a two-way street. The following are a few tips for keeping friendships on track:

- Be aware of your friends' likes and dislikes.

- Remember your friends' birthdays and anniversaries.
- Take interest in your friends' children.
- Become sensitive to their needs.
- Keep in touch with them by phone.
- Express what you like about your relationship with another person.
- Serve your friends in thoughtful, unexpected ways.[21]

Good friends are gifts from God. Is there someone you need to call today?

Friendship is a plant which must often be watered.

GERMAN PROVERB

DR. SIMPSON
AND DANCING

Lively music filled the air as the college students mingled with one another, shared laughs, and danced together. Just then, Dr. Simpson walked up to Rob and asked him, "Why aren't you out there dancing with everyone else?"

"I don't want anyone to laugh at me," he responded.

"What makes you think that they would be looking at you anyway?" came her quick retort with more than a hint of laughter in her voice. She was like that—quick to challenge her students' assumptions, but in a way that provoked thought and self-examination rather than pain and embarrassment.

> He hath put in his heart that he may teach.
>
> EXODUS 35:34
> KJV

A respected and admired professor of English, Dr. Simpson expected much from every student. She was tough, but her classes were always full. It was exchanges like this one that made it possible for Rob to see his life from a perspective other than his own, and in gaining this insight he became more self-confident and less uptight. She helped—no, she forced him to grow as both a student and a person. Dr. Simpson epitomized the role of teacher.

In the words of one author, "The teacher must be able to discern when to push and when to comfort, when to chastise and when to praise, when to challenge and when to hold back, when to encourage risk and when to protect."[22] This, Dr. Simpson did on a daily basis. And, this is just the type of teacher we need. God usually provides each of us with our own unique Dr. Simpson — many times with more than one.

Can you recall your favorite teachers? And, did they challenge you to become more than you were before? Thank God, they did!

A good word costs no more than a bad

one.

ENGLISH PROVERB

BASKET OF LOVE

Every Thursday Jean, a senior citizen, hustled off to visit the people on her list. Some resided in nursing homes; others were lonely at home. Thankful she could still drive, Jean filled a wicker basket with bananas or flowers and sometimes included a cassette tape of her church's Sunday service. Most of all, she packed her basket with lots of love and concern for others.

> Gray hair is a crown of splendor; it is attained by a righteous life.
>
> PROVERBS 16:31

Jean often sat at the bedside of one feeble lady. Although the woman did not respond, Jean treated her tenderly as though she heard and understood every word. She chatted about current happenings, read Scripture, prayed, then kissed her goodbye at the end of the visit and said, "I'll see you next week."

As Jean's friends began to pass away, she felt lonesome for them, but she never stopped serving the Lord. She just found new friends and kept sharing God's love until He called her home.

Like a sturdy basket used for a variety of practical needs, Jean filled her heart and life with love for others. With time and heavy use, baskets may wear out, but God continues to use His children to help others as long as we are willing to carry around His love. Whether we minister to others through praying, meeting physical needs, sending cards, or just calling them on the phone, we can still serve.

Jean didn't just believe in God; she lived her faith by sharing her basket of God's love with all those around her.

———————————————

But with every deed you are sowing a
seed, though the harvest you may not see.

ELLA WHEELER WILCOX

THE CELEBRITY GARDEN

Cherry had finally cleaned a spot in her back yard for a rose garden—her dream for many years. As she thumbed through a rose catalog, she sighed at the magnitude of her choices. *Just like a Christmas wish list,* she thought. *Which ones should I pick? A white John F. Kennedy, a large, pink Peggy Lee, a red Mr. Lincoln, the delicate Queen Elizabeth rose?*

> I am a rose of sharon . . . like a lily among thorns is my darlin among the maidens.
>
> SONG OF SONGS 2:1-2

Sherry closed her eyes as if in deep thought. Suddenly, she had an idea, *I'll plant my own celebrity garden.*

The next day Sherry hurried to her local nursery and bought a dozen roses— all colors and sizes. She worked hard that week, carefully planting each rose. Finally, her task was done, and she decided to throw a party and invite all her friends to help her celebrate her celebrity rose garden.

Imagine their surprise when her friends watched Sherry unveil the celebrity names she had placed on each rose. One by one, they read their own names beside the flowers. The celebrities in Sherry's garden were none other than her friends. But in the middle of the fragrant bouquet, one rose still remained a mystery.

She unveiled the label which read, "Rose of Sharon" and said, "This One is the Love of my life, and everything

QUIET MOMENTS WITH GOD for WOMEN

else centers around Him."

A thousand "celebrities" cry out for our time and attention. Relationships, like a healthy garden, need ample doses of love and affirmation. When Christ is at the center of our affection, all other loves will fall in place.

In the garden of your life, who are your celebrities?

He who would have beautiful roses in his garden must have beautiful roses in his heart.

DEAN HOLE

LARKSPUR LIVES

P auline misread the instructions for planting larkspur seeds and placed the seeds too close together. When the larkspurs emerged from the soil, they looked like a tiny hedge of carrot tops. They seemed so whimsical; she didn't have the heart to thin them as much as perhaps she should have.

Despite her haphazard gardening procedures, Pauline found that the larkspur sprouted and grew in abundance. When a slight breeze ruffled through them, she was sure she heard tiny giggles of joy because the larkspurs knew God had created their beauty.

Their tall flower stalks formed a chorus of pink, blue, white, purple, and occasional splashes of lilac singers. The larkspur choir sang a new song of praise that delighted Pauline's soul. Flowers have the delightful capacity to sing songs for the eyes instead of the ears. The larkspurs stood tall and straight like vertical musical staffs filled with trills of colored notes all the way up their stalks.

As Pauline cut the mature ones for drying, even more

Sing to the Lord a new song; sing to the Lord, all the Earth. Sing to the Lord, praise his name; proclaim his salvation day after day. Declare his glory among the nations, his marvelous deeds among all peoples.

PSALMS 96:1-3

larkspurs shot up and bloomed. The flowers were still singing praises in her garden past the first few light frosts of fall.

Our Christian walk can be a larkspur life. We can daily sing praises to our Lord. We can strive to make our lives of faith an observable witness of God's marvelous deeds.

Can others hear you singing?

O for a thousand tongues to sing my
great redeemer's praise!

CHARLES WESLEY

YULE LOG

I t took place around the second week of December every year. Mother would open her cedar chest and gingerly begin to sort through her most prized material possessions. She took such care as she reached inside and one by one removed items that held great meaning to her. Bubble lights, ornaments, tinsel, and many things shiny and fragrant renewed the season year after year.

> Thy name, O Lord, is everlasting, thy remembrance, O Lord, throughout all generations.
>
> PSALM 135:13 NASB

One special item was always placed on the mantel, transforming the home. It was a yule log, covered in artificial hyssop and man-made holly berries. It had a place in the center for a candle. A bright red satin ribbon was attached with a metal staple on the end to enhance its beauty.

Each year, the family had a tradition of discussing the yule log and remembering what each part of the decoration meant. The log signified a celebration, the birth of Christ. Hyssop, a fragrant herb, was used in ancient Hebrew sacrifices. The lovely red satin ribbon signified the blood of Christ that was shed for our sins. The holly berries represented growth, a bountiful supply. And the candle glowed as a loving reminder that Christ is the Light of the World.

Sometimes in the ordinary, sometimes in our traditions, sometimes in our celebrations, we can find the foundation of our faith. Here, a plain log, a few faded green leaves, some old berries, and a tattered ribbon tell the ageless story of God's infinite love.

God's love for us is proclaimed with each sunrise.

UNKNOWN

FLOWER POWER

B utchart Gardens is one of the most famous tourist attractions in Victoria, British Columbia. The elaborate display dates back to 1904 when Jenny Butchart decided to transform part of her husband's limestone quarry into a sunken garden. Today it is open all year and includes a botanical array of breathtaking beauty.

When one walks through these delightful grounds, it is impossible to choose the most outstanding exhibition. The plants are obviously healthy and well attended. Each provides colorful blossoms that are distinct, yet make a significant contribution in the overall scheme and design.

Likewise, part of our spiritual growth is to realize our importance in God's garden, especially when we exercise the talents and abilities He has given. Many feel inferior about their own gifts, and they compare themselves unfavorably with others. And yet God designs different people just as He created various kinds of flowers. The lily and the rose each have their own features.

We dare not make ourselves of the number, or compare ourselves with some that commend themselves: but they measuring themselves by themselves, and comparing themselves among themselves, are not wise.

2 CORINTHIANS 10:12 KJV

In fact, every blossom has its own unique characteristics. Tulips and lilacs and hyacinths are not alike, and yet each kind of flower adds a particular fragrance and beauty to any arrangement.

The same is true in life. Take a few moments to make an inventory of your gifts. Then ask the Holy Spirit to guide you. Through His power, you can make a difference in the lives of others as well as your own.

The real tragedy of life is not in being limited to one talent, but in the failure to use the one talent.

EDGAR W. WORK

SPONTANEOUS LOVE BOUQUETS

M elanie read the suggestions carefully. "Place contrasting colors together, like peach with blue. Or try red, white, and blue, for a bright, patriotic bed. If you prefer, naturalize your bulbs, incorporating them into your yard's natural habitat. This works particularly well if you live in a wooded, grassy area."

> "Freely you have received, freely give."
>
> MATTHEW 10:8

She grabbed her gardener's tools and set to work, planting some in circles and others in rows. Melanie reserved a handful of varied size bulbs, and like a mother hiding Easter eggs for her expectant child, she tossed bulbs randomly on the grass. Wherever they landed, she carved a hole and dropped them in the ground.

Weeks passed, and Melanie forgot about the bulbs — including their secret hiding places. One early spring day, she walked out in her back yard and saw green shoots poking through the earth. In the next few weeks, her yard looked like a magical wonderland. As she strolled through the green terrain, she realized the most fun part was seeing the bulbs pop up among the natural setting — beside trees, in the middle of a grassy slope, or tucked away in a corner. Nature had worked its magic and rewarded Melanie's long-forgotten efforts with a harvest of beautiful flowers.

Christlike deeds are like the bulbs in Melanie's garden. Some we plant in deliberate, orderly fashion. Others, because of the God-nature planted within us, spill out from our lives naturally like spontaneous love gifts to those around us. These colorful bouquets spring up in the most unexpected places, a true "God-thing," blessing us — and others — in a most beautiful way.

No snowflake ever falls in the wrong

place.

ZENO

WILDFLOWER WORTH

Each spring, wildflowers bloom in profusion at a place in Idaho called "Craters of the Moon." Nourished by snowmelt and occasional rains, the flowers spring up in the lava rock left by an eons-old volcano. It is a stunning sight to see the small, delicate wildflower blossoms bursting into life amid the huge, rugged boulders.

Sightseers can follow footpaths all through the lava rocks to discover the surprising spots that dusty maiden, dwarf monkey flower, and Indian paintbrush find to grow. The life span for the fragile flowers can be as brief as one day if the hot desert winds blow into the area. Even without the winds, three weeks is about their longest show.

When Jesus taught His followers, He often sat outside. Perhaps He sat on a Judean hillside among the spring wildflowers when He pointed at the lilies, encouraging the worriers not to be blinded to the fact that God takes care of all His creation, even a short-lived wildflower. If

"Look at the lilies and how they grow. They don't work or make their clothing, yet Solomon in all his glory was not dressed as beautifully as they are. And if God cares fo wonderfully for flowers that are here today and gone tomorrow, won't he more surely care for you?"

LUKE 12:27-28 NLT

He takes care of them, He certainly will care for us.

How do we avoid worry? By increasing our faith in our God who loves us. By starting each day focusing on Him instead of our fears. And by remembering His loving care even for the brief life of a wildflower.

A day of worry is more exhausting than a day of work.

SIR LOHN LUBBOCK

LIFE LESSONS

Y ou know that what you did was wrong, don't you? The words echoed in Sandra's mind as she went home from school that evening. She was a good student who had never cheated in her life. Yet, this last assignment had been more than she could do. In a moment of desperation, she copied the work of another student.

Speaking the truth in love.

EPHESIANS 4:15
KJV

Her teacher, Mrs. Wallace, had asked her to wait after class, and Sandra knew what was coming. Still, it was a shock when Mrs. Wallace asked her if it was really her work.

"Yes," she squeaked out, then wondered why she had lied.

Looking her straight in the eye, Mrs. Wallace carefully said, "You know that what you did was wrong, don't you? Take tonight to think about your answer, and I will ask you again in the morning if this is your work."

It was a long night for Sandra. She was a junior in high school with a well-deserved reputation for honesty and kindness. She had never cheated before, and now she had compounded her mistake by deliberately lying—and to someone she admired and loved. The next morning she was at Mrs. Wallace's classroom door long before school officially started, and she quietly confessed her misdeed. She received the appropriate consequences, a zero on the assignment and a detention (her first and only detention).

Years later, Sandra often thought of that experience and felt gratitude for loving correction from someone she respected. Mrs. Wallace was willing to help Sandra make honest choices—even on the heels of making a dishonest one. For Sandra, this was a life lesson about taking responsibility for past mistakes and choosing honesty no matter what the consequences.

Honesty is the first chapter of the book
of wisdom.

THOMAS JEFFERSON

A FIRM FOUNDATION

The world's tallest tower stands in Toronto, Ontario, Canada. The first observation deck rises to 1,136 feet, and the second is even higher at 1,815 feet. Photographs and information located inside the tower help visitors comprehend the enormous undertaking of the project. Sixty-two tons of earth and shale were removed from fifty feet into the ground for laying the concrete that rises to the sky.

> "The rain came down, the streams rose, and the winds blew and beat against that house; yet it did not fall, because it had its foundation on the rock."
>
> MATTHEW 7:25

From 1972 to 1974, three thousand workers were at the tower site. Harnessed by safety ropes, some of the laborers dangled outside the giant for their finishing work. Remarkably, no one sustained injuries nor died on location.

Today a rapid elevator transports visitors upward for a breathtaking view of the city and all surrounding areas. Many feel it was well worth the money, time, and effort required to build the CN Tower.

We, too, need a good foundation for facing life each day. As we pray and spend time with our Heavenly Father, we are strengthening our spiritual foundation, our support base for life. We are able to see more from His point of view and not just our own. Thus we are not overwhelmed by whatever comes our way. When we feel we're hanging on the edge or suspended in mid-air, we can take courage in knowing He is holding us—firmly planted—in the palm of His hand. His foundation is strong and sure, and He will not crumble and fall.

Our strength grows out of our weakness.

RALPH WALDO EMERSON

FLOWER-BOX FAITH

One Labor Day weekend, Shannon's husband constructed a large flower-box for her. With great care, she picked out and purchased two hundred top-quality bulbs. Next, she filled the flower-box with the perfect mixture of soil, fertilizer, and peat moss. Then, she spent hours planting the bulbs in a delightful design.

All through the long Idaho winter, she thought about her tulips, daffodils, and hyacinths. If they followed God's plan and waited for His perfect timing, they would change from dull, brown clumps into colorful celebrations of spring.

Maintaining our faith in God during times of forced inactivity is similar to a dormant bulb planted in a flower-box. At certain times in our lives, we may be compelled to stop all activity and take time out to heal. Instead of lying in our beds fretting about our restraining circumstances, we simply need to wait and rest.

Dormancy for a bulb is nature's solution to getting through times of difficult weather conditions. God's gift

On my bed I remember you; I think of you through the watches of the night. Because you are my help, I sing in the shadow of your wings. My soul clings to you; your right hand upholds me.

PSALMS 63:6-8

of rest is His way of helping us through difficult health conditions. All bulbs store food to carry them through their dormant periods. We can use our times of dormancy to nourish our souls by planting our hearts in the fertile soil of His Scriptures.

Like bulbs waiting for spring, we can rest in God's promises as we wait for our recovery. We can look forward to the certain celebration of life through Christ. He alone will bring the colors of spring to our souls.

Simply wait upon him. So doing, we shall
be directed, supplied, protected, corrected,
and rewarded.

VANCE HAVNER

COMFORT IN THE VALLEY

> Even though I walk through the valley of the shadow of death, I fear no evil; for thou art with me; thy rod and thy staff, they comfort me.
>
> PSALM 23:4
> NASB

Several years ago, after the untimely death of her youngest son, Fran had to learn about trusting God. Sometimes she felt forsaken, lonely, and at times even angry that God allowed her seventeen-month-old to succumb to bacterial meningitis. Everything medically possible was done to no avail.

With time, God comforted her with the knowledge that her son is with Him and will be reunited with her someday. The Lord had called Fran to encourage others, even in the midst of her own pain and doubt, and help them understand that while our loved ones will always be in our hearts, our focus remains on the Lord Jesus Christ.

Fran had often read Psalm 23, but she never actually understood it until she visited Israel and saw the rugged terrain traversed by David and the shepherds. Many of the crevices on the rocky hills are so narrow and deep that the sun never shines all the way to the bottom. It remains a shadow. Certain death would result if anyone should fall in, because rescue would be virtually impossible. David's staff helped him walk with sure footing, and the rod defended him from wild animals. Most of all, he became acutely aware of God's provision.

Through the valley times in our lives, we, too, can be sure that we are not alone. His presence is real. Jesus will still be there through all the pain and the changes in our life situations. Nothing is more comforting.

God is closest to those whose hearts are broken.

JEWISH PROVERB

BUMPER CROP

Dorothy wasn't allowed to plant a garden outside the townhouse they rented, so she decided to do the next best thing. She bought large pots and created a container garden on her patio. One evening while she relaxed on the patio, her husband said, "Look! Our neighbor has tomatoes already. Why don't we?"

Much to her amazement, her neighbor had an abundance of fat green tomatoes covering her vines. All that Dorothy had growing were the tiny yellow flowers that promised fruit.

Dorothy had babied her plant by gently positioning it up the rungs of its tomato cage as it grew. She had judiciously showered it with water and had moved the pots around for the best sunshine. Yet, all she had was a profusion of vines.

> Do not be interested only in your own life, but be interest in the lives of others. In your lives you must think and act like Christ Jesus.
>
> PHILIPPIANS 2:4-5 NCV

Dorothy searched through her gardening books and discovered that she needed to pinch back staked tomato plants. Pinching helps the plant focus its energy on producing its fruit instead of merely growing taller.

Many of us are like Dorothy's tomato plant. We love showing the abundant leaves of our spiritual insights. We take pride in how we are climbing the rungs of increased Bible knowledge. But do we only promise fruit, or do we apply what we've learned to our actions? Do we focus our energy on producing quality fruit?

When we pinch back our self-centeredness and concentrate on Christ, we might even grow a bumper crop of fruit to God's glory.

Self is the only prison that can ever bind
the soul.

HENRY VAN DYKE

WHEN FAITH FLUTTERS

Early one morning, Jill sat at her desk sorting through the previous day's bills. Warm rays of spring sunshine streamed through her bedroom window, where she could view the backyard garden.

Out of the corner of one eye, Jill noticed a small, brownish butterfly go by—or so she thought. A few seconds later she turned to look at the window and saw that same butterfly had not landed on a plant; yet it seemed strangely suspended in midair. Its wings fluttered helplessly, but the flying insect could not move.

> You who are spiritual should restore him gently.
>
> GALATIANS 6:1

Puzzled, Jill walked outside to get a closer look. Glistening in the sun, like a ladder of dew-dropped pearls, hung an almost invisible net. During the night, another one of nature's creatures—and one of the butterfly's enemies—had spun a magical web to trap its victims.

Jill observed the struggle briefly until she watched the butterfly's wings grow motionless. She reached over and very gently plucked the winged insect from the spider's deadly threads. At first, the butterfly seemed stunned and fell to the ground. Jill gingerly picked it up and lifted it toward the sky, releasing its wings again. This time, it soared into the air and over the fence.

Anyone can tumble into tangled webs of deception.

We believe a lie, follow the wrong leader, or confuse our priorities. Disillusionment sets in. Tired of the struggle, with faith fluttering, we can easily lose the strength to fight. At that point, a gentle, steady hand may be all we need to help free our fragile wings and send us soaring again on our Heavenly way.

———————————————

A lie travels around the world while truth
is putting her boots on.

FRENCH PROVERB

FLOWERS OF BLESSINGS

Bill and Casey's grades were so close that the faculty asked them both to speak on graduation night at Valley High School. In his speech, Bill prided himself in being self-made. For twenty minutes he enumerated his successes and honors throughout high school. He ended by emphasizing how much he deserved this honor.

> How can we thank God enough for you in return for all the joy we have in the presence of our God because of you?
>
> 1 THESSALONIANS 3:9

A quiet, soft-spoken student, Casey thanked each teacher who had contributed to her high school education. Then she named friends and family members who had influenced her and encouraged her through many discouraging times. "These people are the real stars," she said. "They believed in me when I had no faith. They wished me success when I could not dream. But most of all, I thank my God who has given me grace to come this far."

She continued, "With friends, loved ones, and God's help, you, too, can live your dream. Next year I will enter college and prepare to teach. Although I often wanted to quit, these heroes never did. I can never repay them for their generosity and kindness."

As a close friend gently pushed Casey in her wheelchair down the ramp, the entire student body gave Casey a standing ovation.

Oswald Chambers says, "Whenever you get a bless-ing from God, give it back to Him as a love-gift . . . if you hoard it for yourself, it will turn into spiritual dry rot . . . a blessing . . . must be given back to Him so that He can make it a blessing to others."

Like a grateful gardener, Casey had taken her "flow-ers" of blessings and presented them back to the ones who helped her grow them.

Kindness is the sunshine in which virtue

grows.

ROBERT GREEN INGERSOLL

ONE LONELY SEEDLING

One fall, Margaret decided to dig out a flowerbed by her front door. After the first killing frost, she yanked out the alyssum, tugged out the zinnias, and hauled the cosmos to the compost heap. Then she added fertilizer and mixed it into the dirt with her rototiller.

The following April, as Margaret cleared out the debris that winter winds had blown into the flowerbed, she discovered a solitary cosmos seedling struggling to grow in a corner. The leggy and weak-stemmed cosmos leaned toward the sun in a pathetic call for help. Margaret couldn't imagine how the cosmos seed managed to germinate after all her fall digging.

Margaret transplanted the single seedling into another bed with other baby cosmos. The flower grew strong and radiant within the cosmos congregation.

> Let us not give up meeting together, as some are in the habit of doing, but let us encourage one another.
>
> HEBREWS 10:25

Like the one lonely seedling, we can't reach our full potential alone. Without being joined to a body of believers, spiritual growth can be one-sided or erratic. The transplanted cosmos worked with the other flowers to attract bees and butterflies. This made it possible for each flower to benefit. In the same way, believers are responsible for helping and encouraging each other for the benefit of all.

Joining with others strengthens our faith, expands our experiences, and refreshes our souls. This keeps us spiritually healthy. When we feel isolated or when we pull away from others, perhaps our lonely seedling needs a gentle transplanting.

Blessed is the influence of one true loving
soul on another.

VICTOR HUGO

A GARDEN FAIR

When Pat's daughter needed financial support to do mission work in Hong Kong, she had an idea. Why not host a "Country Garden Fair," charge admission, and give the proceeds to the mission trip? Four hundred guests showed up to enjoy the breathtaking beauty of poppies, larkspur, delphiniums, hollyhocks, and other flowers in her four-acre English country garden. A year later at a second fair, the number of guests tripled. Pat honored her initial commitment and gave the proceeds to missions.

Later Pat took advantage of the high interest in her garden to hold an evangelistic outreach event. She desired that unbelievers would meet God and that existing believers would have a closer walk with Him. Guests admired the brightly colored flowers while listening to hymns and classical music, reading Scripture verses posted along the trails, and soaking up the peace and serenity of God's creation. The Garden Fair, which began as a way to meet a need, flourished as a creative way of planting spiritual seeds in numerous lives.

Because life began in the first garden with Adam and Eve working the soil, we almost feel a pull to return to our roots. In a mysterious way, we feel at home when we dig and plant. Because of Pat's love for gardens, for God, and for people, many others can now also look forward to someday strolling the grounds of their Heavenly home.

How far that little candle throws its beams! So shines a good deed.

WILLIAM SHAKESPEARE

CARROT HEARTS

When Peggy she knew she needed moved from Missouri to Idaho, information about gardening in the mountains.

"Your safest bet is the root crops," a native Idahoan told her. "Potatoes, beets, onions, carrots, those kind of veggies."

Taking his advice, Peggy planted her regular eight-inch carrot seeds totally unaware of the problems that lurked underground. She didn't know stones constantly pushed their way up through mountain soil. She thought her neighbors were joking when they said, "It's a great place to garden. We even grow rocks!"

When Peggy harvested her carrots, she made a disappointing discovery. Her poor carrots had pushed and twisted their way around the rocks trying with all their little carrot hearts to grow. Most of them came out of the ground looking like bright orange corkscrews.

As she tossed her curiously shaped carrots into a bucket, Pauline thought of people whose public appearance came across as just right, but who exposed their

"The good man brings good things out of the good stored up in his heart, and the evil man brings evil things out of the evil stored up in his heart. For out of the overflow of his heart his mouth speaks."

LUKE 6:45

twisted hearts whenever they spoke.

She wondered, Are my words good things that I've stored up, or are they harmful? Do I encourage others and speak words of truth that I've planted in my heart through daily times in God's Word? Or, are my words destructive, coming from a critical heart?

She quietly asked God to help her to honestly confront the harmful rocks hidden in her heart. She was willing to examine herself and make changes, but she was acutely aware of her need for God's help. On her knees in the garden was the perfect place to start.

Nothing is impossible to a willing heart.

JOHN HEYWOOD

ONE HUNDRED YEARS!

W hile Cheryl organized her newly arrived seed order, she found a bonus seed packet containing cactus seeds. She flipped the envelope over to read the planting instructions: "Seeds will germinate in one to one hundred years."

"One hundred years!" she exclaimed aloud. "It would take a wheelbarrow full of faith to sow those seeds. But then, faith is what motivates most gardeners. Few of us live to see a tree seedling grow to its fullest potential. We cannot know if we will still be living in the same place when our biennials bloom. Yet we plan, plant, and have faith in our work."

It's been the same for Christians since Jesus gave the "Great Commission" telling us to plant seeds of faith throughout the world. We are part of a team working for God. We may be the person to plant the Gospel seed in someone's heart, or we may be the one to water it. If faith germinates in a heart and a disciple grows, the accomplishment isn't ours but the Holy Spirit's. We may not

My job was to plant the seed in your hearts, and Apollos watered it, but it was God, not we, who made it grow. The ones who do the planting or watering aren't important, but God is important because he is the one who makes the seed grow. The one who plants and the one who waters work as a team with the same purpose.

1 CORINTHIANS 3:6-8 NLT

even be around to enjoy the harvest.

Cheryl planted her cactus seeds, but they still hadn't germinated when she moved two years later. She remembered them often, however, just as she often remembered to pray for the seeds of faith she'd planted in people's hearts.

The smallest seed of faith is better than the largest fruit of happiness.

HENRY DAVID THOREAU

RISE AND SHINE

Janie jolted awake at the sound of her alarm clock. This was her third day waking up in the middle of the night . . . at least it felt like the middle of the night, even though it was actually early morning. She was not at all sure why she went through the trouble. It especially seemed vague and worthless the moments before her head settled back down onto the pillow.

"No!" she yelled at herself, waking up again with a start. She had promised she would do this, and she was going to, even if she went around for the rest of the day with a sleep-deprived, grumpy attitude. Janie stumbled to the bathroom, splashed some water on her face, and carefully traversed the steps. Downstairs, she started a pot of coffee and sat down at the kitchen table. She had originally started doing her devotions on the sofa, only to discover they only lasted the five minutes it took for her to fall asleep again. At the kitchen table, she took out her Bible, her notebook, and a devotional. Her attitude brightened.

> "Take my yoke upon you and learn from me, for I am gentle and humble in heart, and you will find rest for your souls."
>
> MATTHEW 11:29

Once she was up, every moment was worth it. Meeting God in the early morning hours didn't make her grumpy as she always anticipated, but instead it revitalized her and brought her peace. The early morning moments gave her a chance to see the sunrise, to watch an occasional bird, and to enjoy the silence of a world not yet awake. It took a while to convince her body of the benefits of such early rising, but soon it became habit. After a while, the only time she was grumpy was when she missed her morning meeting with God.

God's yoke is light; He is the rest for our souls that we think sleep should bring. Taking the time with our Savior in the early morning hours is better than fine cappuccino and the smell of omelets and bacon. It truly is the best part of our day.

Take heed of still waters, they quick pass away.

GEORGE HERBERT

APPLE PIE PROBLEMS

Peel. Core. Season. Mix. The steps for making Marilyn's favorite apple pie rolled from her fingertips without a pause. The pie crust lay trimmed and ready in the pie pan, awaiting the seasoned filling. Everything looked just fine. Yet as she added a sprinkling of walnuts and placed the top crust in position, a heavy sigh escaped from her lips.

It was probably a good thing that this was a familiar recipe. Marilyn's mind was not on the pie but rather on a troubled relationship with a close friend. No matter how she tried to solve the problem, things only seemed to grow worse. What do I do now? she wondered.

> He who was seated on the throne said, "I am making everything new!"
>
> REVELATION 21:5

As she slid the pie into the oven, Marilyn remembered a speaker at a seminar who encouraged her listeners to keep a prayer journal. The speaker said she usually prayed aloud as she wrote her concerns in a journal, and that simple exercise clarified her problems and helped her keep track of God's answers.

Marilyn picked up a blank book she had been given for Christmas. Sitting at the kitchen table, she began to write a letter to God, pouring out her heart and her hurt about this troubled relationship. Before she knew it, the oven timer sounded, and she sniffed the familiar warm scent of apples filling the room. She closed the cover on several pages of scrawled script.

Surprisingly, her heart felt lighter. She was struck by the similarity between the pie and the prayer journal. Wrapped between two pie-crusts and left to time and the work of the oven, the apples were still apples, but their taste and texture had changed from tart and crisp to sweet and smooth. In the same way, Marilyn had wrapped her concerns between the covers of prayer. As she set the pie on top of the stove, God reassured her that all she needed was to give Him time to work. He would change that soured relationship and make things sweet again.

Friendship is in loving rather than in being loving.

ROBERT SEYMOUR BRIDGES

SCHEDULED REST

Schedules. Sometimes we feel as though we're governed by to-do lists. The kitchen calendar overflows with notations: do this, go here, pick that up, buy this, deliver that, or mail this other thing. And just when we think we're on top of our lives, someone adds a new item to our to-do list.

Researchers say that Americans today are plagued with more stress-related health problems than any other generation in history. Stress is a contributing factor to heart disease and high blood pressure and has been linked to an increase in bad cholesterol and the worsening of arthritis.

> [Jesus] said to them, "Come with me by yourselves to a quiet place and get some rest."
>
> MARK 6:31

How can we keep the daily pressures of life from becoming debilitating stress? God's solution has always been to take a day of rest. Return to the simple pleasures of the kitchen. The kitchen in our great-grandmothers' time was both the center of family activity and the center of rest. Family meals were made and shared around a common table. Conversation was the primary form of entertainment—not the television, radio, or compact disc player with headphones. Comforting aromas greeted family members throughout the day. And nothing could beat the smell of a chicken roasting in the oven for Sunday dinner.

So toss out the bottle of aspirin, and put your daily

planner away for one day each week. Make sure everyone in the family knows that this will be a "scheduled" day of rest. Before you go to bed the night before, use your modern appliances to help give you a jump-start on the day. Pop some dough ingredients in the bread machine and set the timer on the coffeepot. You'll awaken to the smell of freshly perked coffee and freshly baked bread. Those inviting aromas will make you want to linger in the kitchen—to chat, to laugh, to love, and to rest. God—and our great-grandmothers—will be pleased.

Take rest; a field that has rested gives a
bountiful crop.

OVID

FAITH MOVES FORWARD

"Hey! Stop! The sink's going to overflow!" Ken's sharp cry alerted Ginny to the near disaster as he quickly came to her aid and turned off the water. "What were you looking at? Are the squirrels in the bird feeder again?"

> "Men of Galilee," they said, "Why do you stand here looking into the sky?"
>
> ACTS 1:11

Ginny had been staring out the kitchen window, gazing at nothing yet at everything all at the same time, oblivious to what was going on inside the house. "No squirrels. Just wool-gathering, I guess," she replied absentmindedly.

She turned her attention to the dishes in the sink. For days she had been trying to make some sense out of the feelings that were swirling within her. Compared to someone else's problems, Ginny's concerns would seem to be only minor inconveniences, but for her, they were overwhelming. Finances, relationships, work, health, church—no matter where she turned, there were problems, and all of them seemed beyond her control. Tears mingled with the soapsuds as she finished the dishes. Drying her hands, she sat heavily on a kitchen chair and whispered, "Lord, what am I supposed to do?"

And quietly, the answer came. When the disciples witnessed Christ's return to Heaven, they stood gazing into the sky, not knowing what to do. They were paralyzed by the overwhelming responsibility that He had

130

placed on their shoulders to share the Gospel message with the world. It took a gentle shove from one of God's angels to get them moving down the path that had been placed before them, to turn them away from their fears and back to their faith as they followed God's plan for their lives.

Sure enough, just like those disciples, Ginny had been paralyzed by her dread. She asked forgiveness for her fearful focus, and even before she reached the "Amen," she had a direction . . . a pathway. All she needed to do was faithfully follow God's plan. He'd take care of the rest.

What's holding you back from your God-given dreams? Are you afraid? Remember: Fear stands still, but faith moves forward!

They can conquer who believe they can.

RALPH WALDO EMERSON

THE LOST RING

Godliness with contentment is great gain. For we brought nothing into the world, and we can take nothing out of it.

1 TIMOTHY 6:6-7

When Ginger lost the deep-blue sapphire ring that belonged to her mother, she was devastated. The sapphire, surrounded by twenty-three tiny diamonds, had been passed on to her after her mother died that November.

Ginger planned on having the ring sized to fit her smaller hand. For safekeeping, she placed the ring along with other pieces of jewelry into a plastic bag. Following the Christmas holidays, she couldn't find the ring anywhere, and she gradually forgot about it altogether.

As winter turned into spring, a friend planned a garage sale. Ginger decided to donate an old chest of drawers that she no longer needed. Afterwards, she realized that her mother's jewelry had been inside the chest of drawers, and it had been sold.

Fortunately, Ginger's friend had the phone number of the woman who had bought some of the jewelry. Relieved, Ginger called but was shocked when the woman denied having any of the valuable pieces.

Ginger was furious, and resentment began to build. Finally, her husband said, "Try to remember it was only a worldly possession. I know it's hard, Honey, but let it go."

With an aching heart, Ginger eventually turned the situation over to God and prayed for deliverance from her anger.

Two years passed. One day, the woman who bought the jewelry called and said her own mother had died. Suffering with back pain, the woman had been unable to attend her own mother's funeral. She returned the cherished ring to Ginger, as well as some of the other pieces of her mother's jewelry. Within a short time, the woman's back pain began to disappear.

How often we cling to material things! In Philippians 4:12, Paul says, "I have learned the secret of being content in any and every situation." We need to pray for contentment with what we have. It's a sure thing that we'll take nothing with us when we leave![23]

I am always content with what happens,
for what God chooses is better than what
I choose.

EPICTETUS

KITCHEN-SINK LEGACY

Corinna's grandmother never went to seminary, but she sure could preach. From her kitchen-sink pulpit, Grandma would sermonize while she scrubbed the supper dishes. Her congregation of assembled relatives labored alongside her, clearing the table, drying the dishes, and putting away the pots and pans.

> "Do to others as you would have them do to you."
>
> LUKE 6:31

Corinna wanted to be like the neighbor children who gulped down their meals and left their dishes on the table as they flew out the back door to play. But Grandma would have none of that. If Corinna even hinted at wanting to be excused from her chores, Grandma would answer her with, "If you don't work, you don't eat." By the time Grandma finished her sermonizing, it would be dark outside, and Corinna would have to wait until the next day to play with her friends. She quickly learned to do her chores without excuse or complaint; otherwise Grandma would remind her to "do everything without grumbling or complaining."

It seemed Grandma had a saying for every situation. If someone were upset about the treatment they had received from a friend, a clerk, or a neighbor, Grandma answered with, "Do to others as you would have them do to you." Or if she overheard one of the kids hinting that they were considering something naughty, she quickly countered with, "Be sure your sin will find you out."

Only much later did Corinna discover that Grandma's gems of wisdom came from God's Word. Jesus' words to His disciples were Grandma's answer to bad manners. Paul's words to the Thessalonians and the Philippians were Grandma's encouragement for her to do her chores without complaint. And Moses' words to the wandering Israelites were Grandma's disapproval of wrongdoing.

Grandma's example demonstrates that everyday chores can be used as an opportunity to share God's love.

We should behave to our friends as we would wish our friends to behave to us.

ARISTOTLE

THE QUIET TOUCH
OF STILLNESS

A late-night snowfall blanketed the city one Saturday. When everyone awoke on Sunday morning, evergreens were layered with sparkling white icing. The roofs of houses looked as if someone had draped each one with a fluffy quilt.

> In repentance and rest is your salvation, in quietness and trust is your strength.
>
> ISAIAH 30:15

But more striking than the beautiful whitewash was the pervasive stillness. The city noises were gone. No horns honking or dogs barking. No cars screeching or boom boxes blaring. No doors slamming or machines running. Just stillness — quietness.

The quiet didn't last long, however. Soon city snowplows were out, clearing and salting the streets. The sounds of shovels and snowblowers mixed with window scrapers and revving car engines as neighbors began to dig out from the storm. It was not the first snowstorm of the season, nor would it be the last.

But amazingly, that touch of stillness in the morning put everyone in a better mood. Even the coffee tasted better . . . richer . . . warmer. Despite the hard work of clearing the heavy snowfall, neighbors called out greetings to each other across the yards, accompanied by groans and laughter and squeals of delight. Adults and children made angels in the snow or engaged in mock battle in snowball fights. An entire family of snow people soon populated one lawn.

The quiet start to the morning left its imprint on the entire day. The pace slowed for a moment, granting people an opportunity for reflection and allowing neighbors time to connect with others. And when normal activities resumed, some people were even able to hold on to the stillness for a while.

When Monday came, it brought with it all the noise of a busy week. But it also brought the remembrance of God's words to His people — that in quietness and trust they would find strength. Let God's quietness fill a corner of your heart today, and find the joy that can be found in stillness. It's a blessing far better than a snowball fight!

The great mind knows the power of
gentleness.

ROBERT BROWNING

THE EGG TEST

Have you ever tried to read a recipe while you're cracking an egg into a mixing bowl? If you have—and you're not very adept at it—you know it's not a pretty picture. If you don't keep your eyes on the egg, you'll end up with more egg on the counter than in the mixing bowl. Sometimes you may miss the bowl entirely, and the gooey egg makes a mess, running down the front of your kitchen cabinets, spilling onto the floor. Yuck! Any experienced cook will tell you that you'll have better success if you read the recipe first and then keep your eyes on the eggs.

> As the heavens are higher than the Earth, so are my ways higher than your ways and my thoughts than your thoughts.
>
> ISAIAH 55:9

The Bible agrees. Well, maybe it doesn't talk about eggs and mixing bowls, but it does talk about our choices in life. When the Israelites first camped on the edge of the Promised Land, God instructed them to do some reconnaissance. Twelve men were sent to look the land over and report back to Moses with their findings. All twelve had seen God miraculously deliver them from slavery. All twelve had heard God's promise of protection. All twelve had experienced God's provision for their journey.

But only two men remembered God and His faithfulness. Only two kept their focus on God—ten men were distracted by the sights and smells of Canaan. Ten men turned their eyes away from God and made a mess for the Israelites that took forty years to clean up. A glance away from God caused Israel's slippery slide to disobedience.

Whenever we focus on our problems instead of on God's promises and possibilities, we're in for a slippery slide too. The Bible says that God doesn't view things from our limited perspective. If we want the recipe of our lives to turn out for the best, we need to stay focused on Him. Let the egg test be your reminder: Whenever you crack an egg for a recipe, keep your eye on the egg and remember to ask yourself if your heart is focused on God.

By asking for the impossible, we obtain
the best possible.

ITALIAN PROVERB

BEAUTY FOR ASHES

Sitting at her round oak kitchen table, Sharon smiled as she sprayed the glass in the frame with glass cleaner. The words of the inspirational poem she had written for a friend who was facing cancer surgery came into sharp focus. Later, Sharon would take "food for the soul" to her friend.

Looking outside, the gray December day reminded her of a similar day when she was in seventh grade. She could still see her teacher standing at the chalkboard, asking the class to write a poem.

Aware that Christmas was at the doorstep, she began writing. Her poem, so different from those of her classmates, was about the birth of the Christ Child. She took it home and rewrote it until the poem shone as though it were the star of Bethlehem itself.

"This is wonderful," the teacher said the next day. "Did you do this all by yourself?"

Beaming, Sharon said, "Yes, ma'am." Then the teacher read the poem to the entire class. She was beside herself with joy that day.

[He has sent me] to bestow on them a crown of beauty instead of ashes, the oil of gladness instead of mourning, and a garment of praise instead of a spirit of despair.

ISAIAH 61:3

A couple of days later, however, the teacher asked to speak with her in the hall. There, after talking to another teacher, she accused her of stealing the poem from a book. Brokenhearted, Sharon refused to write another poem—until twenty-five years later.

By then, Sharon was a woman who had returned to writing as a form of therapy during some difficult trials. One day, with Christmas again approaching, she wrote several Christmas poems. She sent them off to a publisher, expecting a rejection. Later, she received a letter indicating that two of her poems had been accepted.

Are you neglecting your talents because someone criticized you in the past? Don't let your gifts become ashes; turn them into a crown of beauty for God. Whether it's cooking, serving, speaking, writing, or making something beautiful with your hands, do it for His glory.

He how neglects the present moment
throws away all he has.

JOHANN FRIEDRICH VON SCHILLER

VOICE FROM THE PAST

Laura was mixing cake batter when the phone rang. The voice on the other end said, "Hi. This is a voice from your past."

Since she didn't recognize the voice, Laura quipped, "Whose voice and from which past?"

> Faith by itself, if it is not accompanied by action, is dead. But someone will say, "You have faith; I have deeds." Show me your faith without deeds, and I will show you my faith by what I do.
>
> JAMES 2:17-18

Laughter broke out on the other end. "This is Carrie," she said. Of course, Laura thought. Carrie had been a member of her writer's group. In fact, she had written beautiful and thought-provoking fiction. Her work was good, and she could have been published if she had pursued it. Instead, Carrie chose to end an unhappy marriage and get on with her life, leaving her writing far behind.

Carrie bubbled with excitement. "I'm sailing with friends on a forty-two-foot sailboat from Nova Scotia to Scotland." Laura listened intently. Was this the same Carrie who had needed lots of support from her friends? The same Carrie who had wrapped herself safely in a little shell? To Laura's surprise, Carrie had changed. She was now taking control of her life and doing exciting things. She wasn't the least bit apprehensive about crossing choppy waters, battling seasickness, or running from sharks and killer whales.

As Carrie was closing the conversation, she said, "I wanted to make certain my good friends knew I was going on this trip." Laura's breath caught in her throat. She had never thought of herself as Carrie's good friend. Sure, she'd taken her to the doctor once, visited her apartment, and even lunched at a pizza place with her and her children, but she'd never thought of herself as her good friend. She couldn't even recall her last name.

How often do we touch someone's life with a random act of kindness? God uses ordinary people to make an extraordinary difference in the world around them. Find a way to be kind to another person today.

He who plants kindness, gathers love.

SAINT BASIL

JUST LIKE PAUL

P rior to his conversion, the Apostle Paul persecuted scores of Christians. But God met this
ruthless Pharisee in a special vision on the
road to Damascus and changed his heart.

Yet wherever Paul went after his conversion, he
caused controversy. The book of Acts tells us that many
Christians were unwilling to accept his conversion as a
real change of heart. They feared that his supposed love
for Christ was mere playacting and would ultimately
result in their imprisonment. Jews were angry at his new
message too. Death threats
against him were common-
place, and the increasing
threats of violence prompted
the church leaders in
Jerusalem to take Paul to the
seacoast, place him aboard a
ship, and send him back to his
hometown of Tarsus.

> Encourage one
> another and
> build each other
> up, just as in
> fact you are
> doing.
>
> 1 THESSALONIANS
> 5:11

For several chapters, the
book of Acts is silent about the life of Paul. But when he
reappears in the narrative in Acts 11, no one questions
his change of heart. No one misunderstands his inten-
tions. No one criticizes his involvement in missionary
endeavors. Something is different about Paul.

While the Bible does not tell us what happened to
Paul during that time, perhaps he went home to his family. Think of a time when you returned home after a long

and maybe difficult absence. There's something reassuring about sitting at the same old kitchen table, cooking on the same old stove, listening to the same noises, and smelling the same aromas from your younger days—a simpler time. The four walls of the family home become a place to regenerate and renew. And when it comes time to move on again, you are refreshed and ready—just like Paul.

Whether you're sharing a favorite meal with a family member or a conversation with a friend until the wee hours of the morning, let your home be a haven . . . a place of refreshment. After all, you just might be strengthening another soul for ministry—someone like Paul.

———————

Tell a man he is brave, and you help him
to become so.

THOMAS CARLYLE

SUNBEAM BLESSINGS

As Gloria sat alone at the dining table, a single sunbeam shone through the closed blinds. At the point where the light entered the window, it was just a tiny speck, but as it spread across the room, all the colors of the rainbow burst into an array of splendor. It highlighted the old shadowbox that hung on the wall and reflected on its glass front that protected her treasures from dust and grime.

The crystal ornament inside the box split the sunbeam into a million fragments of color and drew her attention to the other items. She spotted the golden tree figurine covered with her birthstones and thought of how her mother often spoke of what a glorious day it was when she was born. She saw the animal figurines that resembled her pets from long ago. The angel standing over the small boy and girl on the bridge reminded her of her childhood years, as she and her brother played by the creek's edge beside their home.

> "I am the light of the world. Whoever follows me will never walk in darkness, but will have the light of life."
>
> JOHN 8:12

The baby figurine took her back to the days when her children were small. The fellow pointing to a carving in a tree that said, "I Love You," made her smile. It had been a gift from her husband on one of their anniversaries. Many fond memories came alive as Gloria spied the tiny angel holding the Bible, and she thanked God for the many blessings in her life.

Even in the midst of difficult circumstances, try to remember the good things God has done for you, no matter how small or insignificant. It will get your eyes off your problem and on the Solver of problems instead.

———————————

There are no days when God's fountain
does not flow.

RICHARD OWEN ROBERTS

THE GOD OF TOMORROW

When the microwave buzzed, Rebecca slid her chair away from her laptop computer and retrieved the hot water for her tea. She had been writing an article about new technologies and how they would impact our lives in the next century. The whole topic was unsettling. The more research she did on the Internet, the more disturbed she became about cloning, supercomputers, and spy satellites. Where would it all end?

> I am the Lord—I do not change.
>
> MALACHI 3:6 TLB

Suddenly, she had an urge to hear the comforting whistle of a teakettle and the crackling of a real fire instead of the hiss of a gas log. The world was moving too fast, and at times like these, she wanted to crawl up in her grandpa's lap and smell his sweet cherry pipe.

"Grandpa," she remembered asking one time, "did you have spaceships when you were little?"

He chuckled and said, "No, Honey, when I was a little boy, we rode in a horse-drawn wagon to town. And airplanes had just really gotten off the ground."

"But you had trains."

"Yep, I guess I always liked trains the best."

The sound of a train whistle still reminded her of Grandpa and how he looked in his navy-blue conductor's uniform. Sometimes he would let her dress up in it and carry around his big silver watch. "All aboard!" she'd call, and Grandpa would pretend to be a passenger.

I wonder what Grandpa would think about life today? She knew. He'd tell her not to worry. "Honey," he'd say, "I've been in some pretty tight places in my day: train wrecks, labor strikes, and world wars. I reckon if God pulled us through all of that, He can see us the rest of the way home."

She "reckoned" He would. The God of her grandpa's era would be the same God in the twenty-first century. And that was a comforting thought.

God's investment in us is so great he
could not possibly abandon us.

ERWIN W. LUTZER

CHANGING SEASONS

Marie had always enjoyed washing dishes by hand. It gave her an opportunity to slow down, think, and observe the changing of the seasons as she gazed out her kitchen window.

> The grass withers and the flowers fall, but the word of our God stands forever.
>
> ISAIAH 40:8

Over the course of a year, Marie watched a sparrow preparing her nest and then bringing food to her babies in the springtime. A hummingbird made regular stops after he discovered the window feeder during the summer. In autumn, squirrels scampered around in the crisp fallen leaves in search of an acorn. And that winter, Marie saw a deer standing majestically in her yard.

As the cycle of seasons began again, Marie watched flowers pop up through the soil when the weather got warmer. Their brilliantly colored blossoms always brought her happiness. In the summer, the green grass filled her heart with peace and tranquility. And as the green leaves gradually transformed to shades of gold, she sensed the autumn nip in the air, a sure sign that winter would follow.

Life is like the changing seasons. During the springtime of Marie's life, her days were filled with fun and joy as she played with frogs and tadpoles. Her teen and young adult years—the summer of her life—were marked by enthusiasm as she tried to find herself in the fast lane of life. Today, Marie is beginning to sense the contentment of autumn. She sees security in the eyes of her husband and joy in the lives of her grown children, and she realizes that winter soon will be upon her.

As a Christian, Marie knows that one day she will awaken to a world more wonderful than she can even imagine. Until then, she knows that whatever season she's in right now is the best season of her entire life.

There's nothing wrong with looking back at the previous seasons of our lives. But God has a purpose for allowing us to be in the season we're in right now. So enjoy where you're at on the way to where you're going!

As dew to the blossom, the bud to the bee,

as the scent to the rose, are those

memories to me.

AMELIA C. WELBY

MONDAY MORNING MINDSET

On Monday, the television newscaster looked grim as he read the statistics of the latest crime spree. The weatherman predicted a heavy snowstorm with possible ice damage and power outages. The car mechanic indicated that the repairs to the brake system would cost more than expected. The doctor's office called, requesting an immediate appointment to discuss the results of a biopsy.

> Let us continually offer to God a sacrifice of praise.
>
> HEBREWS 13:15

But also on Monday, Grandma went to the oncologist and received a survivor pin commemorating five cancer-free years. Amy pulled through labor and delivery with no complications and gave birth to a healthy little girl. Sam's blood test revealed that he was merely overstressed and overtired, not diabetic. Frank passed a college exam with flying colors. Erin believed she had found someone to marry.

All of these events are part of the routines of daily life and frame the conversations shared around the kitchen table. Sometimes those conversations are punctuated with sniffles and tears. But many times those talks ring loudly with laughter and song. The difference is usually found in our focus.

Concerns and problems are a part of life. Things go wrong. Plans fail. But we have a choice. We can either focus entirely on the problems, or we can focus on God.

A problem-filled focus yields a fearful heart, and fear is a thief that robs us of the joy of today. However, a focus that acknowledges God's control over everything fills our hearts with peace, comfort, and joy despite our problems. We can listen to the newscaster and the weatherman, the mechanic and the physician, but we need to make some time to focus on our daily blessings, too, thanking God for those little reminders of His care.

Rest assured, he is still in control of everything. Tell him about the heartache, and tell him the longings too, tell him the baffled purpose when we scarce know what to do, then, leaving all our weakness with the one divinely strong, forget that we bore the burden and carry away the song.

PHILLIPS BROOKS[24]

THE BETTER WAY

Martha was a dedicated homemaker. She was an expert at entertaining her guests while preparing a scrumptious meal at the same time. One day when Jesus was passing through the village, Martha opened her home to Him. Her house was spotless, and the aroma coming from her kitchen was delightful. As a wonderful hostess, she made sure that Jesus felt welcome in her home.

Her sister, Mary, also was there. While Martha opened her home to Jesus, Mary opened her heart to Him and sat at His feet. She knew that true wisdom would be hers if she listened to His teachings and applied them to her everyday life.

> Since, then, you have been raised with Christ, set your hearts on things above, where Christ is seated at the right hand God.
>
> COLOSSIANS 3:1

Meanwhile, Martha began to grumble. She felt that Mary should be more involved in the work at hand. She went to Jesus to ask Him to send her sister to help her in the kitchen.

Jesus' response probably surprised her. He taught Martha some things about priorities, while sharing with her a better way to serve Him. Mary, He said, had chosen the better way, and it would not be taken away from her.

What are the priorities in your life? Do you take time out of your busy schedule to read God's letter to the world? The Bible holds the key to successful living and abounding happiness. Is your prayer time an important part of your day? Jesus is always available to listen to you. God is never too busy to offer encouragement and love to His children.

While working and serving are vital parts of living, they cannot be the most important parts. Seek God's guidance today through prayer and Bible study. The wisdom that you gain will benefit not only you, but others as well, for your life will serve as a shining example for Him.

Deep in your heart it is not guidance that you want as much as a guide.

JOHN WHITE

SOMEONE WHO CARES

Maureen wearily rinsed out her coffee cup and stacked it in the nearly full dishwasher. Her life had been difficult for months. As her husband's illness rapidly progressed, her sense of security waned, and a fear of losing him filled her heart. After a few weeks in the hospital, her husband of forty-five years was forced to live in a nursing home. It seemed that Maureen couldn't stop crying. Her heart felt heavier after each visit.

> An anxious heart weighs a man down, but a kind word cheers him up.
>
> PROVERBS 12:25

At first, people asked if there was anything they could do to help. Others telephoned and visited her. But after a few weeks, the calls and visits dwindled as her friends got on with their lives. She was overcome with weariness, and joy seemed so remote.

One day before she left for her daily visit to the nursing home, she stopped by the mailbox. A small "thinking of you" card was tucked inside. It was signed, "Someone who cares." A ray of sunshine touched her heart as she read those simple words.

Someone really cares, she thought. She didn't know who it was, but she knew that someone was concerned about the situation that overshadowed her life. All day long she wondered who had been so kind. She looked at the card over and over, trying to see if she could recognize the signature. She knew that the person was praying for her, and she wanted to let her know how much she appreciated it.

As the weeks and months passed, Maureen continued to receive greeting cards from this anonymous person. The signature was always the same. But no one ever confessed to being the sender. Only God knew who uplifted her spirit. And for the sender, that was enough.

Kindness is a language the dumb can

speak, the deaf can hear, and the blind can

see.

UNKNOWN

A CONTINUAL FEAST

Janice could barely look at Minnie. She saw in the aging, lined face before her the haunting call of her own weary bones. Working in a nursing home when she herself was growing older could sometimes bring a deep sadness to Janice's heart. And here she was, watching the end of a life struggle to move down the hallway.

> All the days of the oppressed are wretched, but the cheerful heart has a continual feast.
>
> PROVERBS 15:15

Minnie, Janice's patient, was bent at the waist and shuffling slowly with the use of a walker. Her stiff and gnarled hands were white with the pressure. It took Minnie what seemed like hours to make her way across the small expanse of tile.

Finally, with much effort and painful exertion, Minnie turned and settled into the seat. Janice folded up the walker and leaned it against the wall, feeling her own aches and pains as she did so.

"Janice?" Minnie's voice was barely above a whisper as she beckoned Janice closer.

"Yes, Minnie?"

"Isn't it a beautiful day?"

Janice followed Minnie's line of vision, trying to see what beauty she saw. There was little to notice: a plant, a painting, a few friends. Janice looked into her eyes.

They were bright and capable, even though her body no longer followed suit. Minnie knew exactly what she was saying when she commented on the beauty of the day. Janice had to smile as she replied, "Yes, Minnie, it's a beautiful day."

Is there an ache or pain you can set aside today to see the good? Is there something that's holding you back or that seems insurmountable? When you look beyond your circumstance, is there beauty there? Pain is real, and it's a struggle when life doesn't cooperate with our plans. But always, there is more. Always, there is something that God will place into our line of vision that is worth celebrating. It doesn't always take away the pain, but as He promises in Proverbs 15:15, "The cheerful heart has a continual feast." Once you start noticing the sublime, He makes it far too good to ever pass up again.

Cheerfulness: the habit of looking at the good side of things.

WILLIAM BERNARD ULLANTHORNE

WRONG ROUTE

L izzy and Karen were in downtown Seattle, sitting in the hotel lobby and waiting for a bus. They had broken free of a conference and were ready to explore the city that surrounded them. They'd been waiting for the bus for twenty minutes and found themselves impatient and eager. There was so much to do . . . so much to see!

> Wait for the Lord; be strong and take heart and wait for the Lord.
>
> PSALM 27:14

Moments later, a bus pulled up. "It's not the one they said we should take," Lizzy said, smiling as she began walking toward the doors, "but it's headed in the same direction! Let's go!" They climbed on board — two Midwestern girls, heading for the sights. As the bus made its way through the dark and scary underbelly of the city, the girls huddled together in a small corner of the bus. The driver seemed amused by their predicament, and their fellow passengers seemed anything but willing to help them find their desired destination. They grasped each other's hands and tried to look less like tourists and more like residents. That only served to emphasize their discomfort.

Lizzy and Karen ended up staying on the bus for the whole route. Arriving back at the hotel, they were slightly shaken and had only lost a little time. They grinned at each other ruefully and waited . . . and waited . . . and waited for the right bus.

Is there a bus you're tempted to climb aboard because you're tired of waiting? Is there a relationship, a job, a direction you're thinking of taking that may not be God's best for you? There is much to be gained by waiting in the lobby for the right bus. God will not abandon you in your search. He is there, ready and waiting with His answer, reminding you of His sovereign will and His ability to take you where you need to go. It's okay to wait on Him. In fact, it's much safer and a whole lot wiser, especially when you consider the alternative.

All comes at the proper time to him who
knows how to wait.

SAINT VINCENT DE PAUL

THE GIFT OF WORDS

Melissa wanted more than anything to be able to sing and play the piano! Unfortunately, she simply had no musical talent, no matter how hard she tried or how much she practiced. She finally came to the conclusion that she had no sense of rhythm and no ability to carry a tune.

Marrying a preacher with a beautiful voice didn't help matters. Everyone knows that the pastor's wife is supposed to play the piano. She had never seen it written in any book, but she saw it written on every church member's face. She hated pastoral interviews, because she knew the dreaded question would come eventually: "Do you play the piano?" She always felt like a failure as she answered that inevitable question with a solemn no.

> There are different kinds of gifts, but the same spirit. There are different kinds of service, but he same Lord.
>
> 1 CORINTHIANS 12:4-5

For years she prayed, "God, give me the ability to sing," but during the congregational hymns, she realized that nothing had happened. Her voice was just as bad as it was before she prayed. She took piano lessons until a well-meaning teacher kindly told her that she was wasting her money. Many times she wondered why God didn't answer her prayer in the way she would have liked.

One day, Melissa started singing for the joy of it and gave up on the idea of being an accomplished pianist or soloist. She sang in the shower after everyone had left for the day and hummed as she cooked before anyone arrived back home in the evening.

She taught Sunday school and later started writing. She discovered the talents that God had given to her had nothing to do with music. He had given her the gift of words. Melissa worked hard at becoming a successful writer and reached many people with her words of encouragement.

God does not give everyone the same talents. We're all unique and special in His eyes. Discovering her talent gave Melissa an entirely different outlook on life. Now when that difficult question arises, she smiles and answers, "No, I don't sing or play, at least not for anyone except the Lord! Instead, He gave me the gift of encouraging others."

A bit of fragrance always clings to the hand that gives you roses.

CHINESE PROVERB

GUILTY SNACKING

Stacie was sitting in her office when she first heard the commotion.

"No way!"

"Check it out!"

"Who's got some quarters?"

Stacie got up from her desk and walked cautiously toward the sound of money and elation. She rounded the corner to discover three of her coworkers gathered around the vending machine. They were inserting change, picking out items, and receiving both the snack and their money back. The machine had a loose wire and was giving out free food.

> "Watch and pray so that you will not fall into temptation. The spirit is willing, but the body is weak."
>
> MARK 14:38

Stacie grinned. No breakfast that morning and quarters in her pocket made for a happy young woman. She pushed her way through the crowd and gave it a try. Three quarters . . . some powdered donuts. Three quarters back . . . a big cinnamon roll. Three quarters back . . . a bag of chips. Carrying her quarters and her unexpected breakfast, she headed back to her desk with a smile on her face.

It wasn't until she sat down that the guilt (and the calories) settled heavily on her conscience. It wasn't right! No matter that everyone else seemed to be okay with it. No matter that the vending machine guy was always grumpy and never stocked the items she liked . . . no matter about any of that! This was wrong. It was stealing, and she couldn't do it.

Oh, but how her stomach growled! Surely it would be okay if she had one bite . . . just one.

Stacie ate it all. But when the vendor came later, she dug into her pocket and paid for all three items. Her coworkers looked at her oddly, but she felt much better.

Sometimes it's easier to ignore the little things that no one else cares about — to join others who believe that if no one knows, it can't possible hurt. Today, take a stand for the little acts of truth . . . the small steps of honesty and courage. Though some may mock you, you just may earn the respect of others, and God will use that to draw them to His heart.

Courage is fear that has said its prayers.

DOROTHY BERNARD

ABOVE THE CLOUDS

Denise rested her flushed face against the cool window. It had been hours since she had left her warm bed to fight her way to the airport. Finally, she sat on the plane, which was preparing to taxi onto the runway.

This trip, unlike many others, brought none of the familiar pleasure to her heart as the plane began to move . . . no vacation . . . no friend's wedding. This trip was a somber one to visit her ailing father in a distant state.

> "My thoughts are not your thoughts, neither are you ways my ways," declares the Lord.
>
> ISAIAH 55:8

Her father was sick; her husband was frustrated and angry as his company transitioned to a younger, more "able" staff; and her teenage son was pushing the envelope to fit in with a group of students Denise feared and disliked. Why was all of this taking place now? Why, Lord? She had prayed! She had always lived a life worthy of blessing and reward—or so she had thought.

As the plane slowly rose into the air, Denise surveyed the land below her. Dark and dreary under a cloudy, rainy sky, the entire landscape seemed to fit her mood. Slowly, the plane began to break through the clouds, and Denise could no longer see the land below. They seemed to be lost in a gray mist until they climbed on top of the clouds. What a difference! The dark, menacing clouds were transformed into soft white blankets. The blue sky and sunshine were bright and unwavering on the other side.

Does life seem dark and dreary from your perspective? Are you living beneath the dark clouds of depression or sadness? It's hard to see the light in the midst of the storm. But remember, just beyond the cloud cover is an amazing sight. Today, allow God to show you life from His perspective.

He that can have patience, can have what he will.

BENJAMIN FRANKLIN

THE GOD FACTOR

Surrounded by stacks of invoices and receipts, Theresa's fingers flew over the number pad of her keyboard, recalculating and checking the year's expenditures and income. She couldn't believe how much money their employees had wasted on copy paper. Still, it looked like they were going to make a good profit for the first time this year. Thank God! she thought wearily. They had finally licked their turnover problem by providing better healthcare coverage and dental insurance.

> "Where your treasure is, there your heart will be also."
>
> MATTHEW 6:21

Theresa picked up her coffee cup and walked down the hall to the small kitchen their company provided. One of her employees sat at the table reading her Bible and eating a microwave dinner.

"What are you doing here so late?" Theresa asked, pouring another cup of coffee.

"Oh, hi, Mrs. Chase," Angela said. "I thought I'd work tonight and get out that report you needed by tomorrow afternoon."

"You don't have to do that," Theresa said.

"I know, but I just wanted to double check my figures."

"I appreciate all your hard work."

"Thanks," Angela said, smiling and closing her Bible.

"And thanks for letting us start a Bible study group in the morning. We've been praying for you and the business too."

"It's working!" Theresa said. "Keep it up."

Instead of the conventional wisdom, which says that a business should only make decisions based on the bottom line, the relationship between an employer and an employee is a symbiotic one. It takes a cooperative effort to achieve success. Some companies finally are realizing that there is a "God factor" at work when a business cares sincerely for its employees and sows appreciation as well as benefits into their lives. If you are a businessperson, consider allowing your employees to start a Bible study or prayer group during lunchtime or before or after work. Invite God into your workplace, and He will honor your trust in Him.

A wise man will make more opportunities
than he finds.

FRANCIS BACON

A HEART OF HOSPITALITY

B ecause of Jeff's profession, he and Rochelle relocated many times over the years. However, one of the relocations was memorable, not because of something that happened, but rather because of something that didn't happen.

Jeff was required to begin his position in a new city before their home was ready for occupancy. A woman from a local church heard about his predicament and offered him the use of her family's guest room until their home was ready.

> When Priscilla and Aquila heard him, they invited him to their home and explained to him the way of God more adequately.
>
> ACTS 18:26

When they finally moved into their new house, Rochelle wanted to show her gratitude to the woman for her kindness to Jeff. She called and asked her to stop by for tea, apologizing that she'd probably have to sit on a few packing boxes but assuring her that she would be most welcome. There was a slight pause before the woman replied, "No, dear. I won't come over just now. I'll wait until you have things the way you want them. Then we can have a nice visit."

The woman was no doubt only trying to give Rochelle some extra time to settle in. But things didn't quite work out the way she thought they would. Rochelle never seemed to get things "the way she wanted them." Some of the living room packing boxes stayed in the dining room for a few months, as they waited for repairs to be made to the living room floor. Then when those boxes were emptied, the dining room disintegrated into a mess of wallpaper, paint, and floor tile samples for the kitchen. By the time those things were taken care of, nine months had gone by, and Rochelle was too embarrassed to re-extend her invitation of hospitality.

A hospitable person is gracious, cordial, and generous. Hospitality asks us to open our hearts to others, whether our homes are picture perfect or not. And when we refuse hospitality, we may be hurting the heart of a stranger. Let's keep our hearts open to give and receive hospitality. We're sure to find God's blessings — and quite possibly a friend too.

When there is room in the heart there is room in the house.

DANISH PROVERB

THE GOD WHO NEVER SLEEPS

I n March of 1975, a tornado raked an eight-mile path across Atlanta, Georgia, snapping pine trees like toothpicks. Civil defense officials estimated the damage to be as high as thirty million dollars.

Even today, Gloria remembers that day as though it were yesterday. She was a younger woman then and was working part-time as a secretary at a small office. The office was closed that Monday so employees could attend a memorial service for a coworker.

That morning as Gloria got ready for the service, she noticed the skies outside turn an ominous black. The wind picked up, and trees bowed like rubber. She watched metal garbage cans being tossed down the street. Then the driving rain hit. The last thing on Gloria's mind, though, was a tornado.

> Cast all your anxiety on him because he cares for you.
>
> 1 PETER 5:7

After attending the service, she drove home. Visibility was poor as the rain slanted in sheets across the road. When she passed by her office, she almost wished she had gone to work, so she wouldn't have to battle the weather all the way home. The constant scraping of the windshield wipers grated on her nerves, so she turned on the radio to drown out the sound. The news reports were unbelievable! A tornado had been spotted in the Atlanta area. She accelerated, urging her car toward home.

QUIET MOMENTS WITH GOD for WOMEN

Not until later did she learn that the tornadoes that whipped through Atlanta had destroyed the building where she worked. When she finally went back to the office and surveyed the damage, she found everything in shambles. She trembled when she saw the collapsed concrete wall on top of her desk and shuddered to think what might have happened had she gone to work.

What a blessing to know that God is omnipresent! He is the One who neither slumbers nor sleeps. He promises to be with us and deliver us even in the midst of a whirlwind. Look to God when darkness blankets your world, and He will show you the way home!

To worry about tomorrow is to be
unhappy today.

PROVERB

HIDDEN BEAUTY

Shortly after the New Year arrived, Brenda noticed the clutter on her dining-room table. She thought of the Christmas celebration just a few weeks earlier and how beautiful her table had been as she welcomed church members into her home. Just being with her friends made the evening special.

O Lord, our Lord, how majestic is your name in all the earth!

PSALM 8:9

Now life was back to normal. The tree was packed up, and the nativity scene had been put away. The elegant setting had been removed from her table and replaced with several bills that needed to be paid. Contributing to the jumble was a box of tissues (the remnant of a bout of pneumonia that had slowed her pace during the holidays) and an address book.

Brenda picked up the address book and flipped through the pages. Each page was filled with names, addresses, and telephone numbers. She realized that this book represented her family and friends, and she thought about how fortunate she was to have so many people who loved her. As she read the names, she offered up a prayer for each one. She prayed for their special needs and asked God to walk with them daily.

She picked up the tissues and thanked God for her health. Then she looked over the bills and thanked God for her career and the opportunity to provide for her family. One by one, she counted her many blessings.

At first glance, the things on Brenda's table seemed to invade the beauty of her home, but as she looked at each item, she realized that each one served as a reminder of God's presence in her life.

If men thanked God for good things, they wouldn't have time to complain about the bad.

JEWISH PROVERB

THE KINGDOM FAMILY

Charlene walked down the aisle alone. This had been the moment she was supposed to share with her father—the precious time when he would give his blessing to her marriage and officially hand her over, as she made the transition from daughter to wife.

Yet her father was not there. Nor was her mother or sister. Her family had a previous commitment, a convention they had to attend, and that convention had been more important than her wedding. It had been a tough blow, and Charlene could feel the pain clouding this special moment.

> "Whoever does the will of my Father in heaven is my brother and sister and mother."
>
> MATTHEW 12:50

There, waiting at the altar, was her pastor—her shepherd. His warm and tender smile received them into his presence. Charlene felt her longing subside as she looked into his kind face. The pastor and his wife had been better than family. They had counseled, laughed, and cried with Charlene as she worked through premarital jitters. They had prayed with her and held her hand. They were more father and mother to her than her biological parents had ever been.

Charlene smiled from the depths of her heart at her waiting bridegroom. This was a time to celebrate the new, and God had been faithful in surrounding her with parents, brothers, and sisters that were part of His kingdom.

Have you lost your family? God is faithful in providing people who will nurture us, love us, and fill the empty spaces in our lives. Your family doesn't have to come from the same womb or share the same blood. Allow Him to give you the gift of His family. We are meant to be that for each other.

The Lord gives his blessing when he finds
the vessel empty.

THOMAS A KEMPIS

LIGHT AND FLUFFY

"W hat's that, Grandma?" the little girl asked, as she watched her grandmother carefully mix the ingredients for bread.

"Yeast," Grandma replied. "That's what makes the bread rise. We have to cover the dough with a cloth and put it in a warm place if we want our rolls to be light and fluffy."

Not fully understanding the way yeast works, Mary was impatient. She continued to lift the cloth in order to see the round balls of dough that sat in the baking dish. After a while, she realized that they were growing larger.

Finally, Grandma placed the rolls in the preheated oven. Mary watched through the glass window as the tops began turning golden brown. The scent permeated the whole house. When the rolls were done, Mary was allowed to brush a small amount of butter on the top of each one.

Mary's grandmother thought about the look of amazement on her granddaughter's face when she saw how the bread had doubled in size. Her own faith, she real-

"What shall I compare the kingdom of God to? It is like yeast that a woman took and mixed into a large amount of flour until it worked all through the dough."

LUKE 13:20-21

ized, was a lot like that dough. The more she prayed and studied God's Word, the larger her faith grew. And just as the rolls needed to remain warm in order to rise, she needed to keep her heart warm in order to serve God and others.

Today, keep a warm smile on your lips and a glow in your eyes. With a "light and fluffy" attitude toward life, we can rise up in the midst of trouble and show others the warmth that only God can provide.

Remember, the faith that moves
mountains always carries a pick.

UNKNOWN

CLOSING THE DOOR

Michelle looked around her office and felt a sigh rise from the depths of her soul. She had worked so hard for all of this and had put so many hours into her vision, especially at the beginning, when her company had only been a dream and her energy was committed to making it a reality. Someone else had appreciated her creativity—a bigger, larger company that had bought her out in a forceful merger. Now all that was once hers belonged to an unseen face. It was like losing a family member.

> We want each of you to show this same diligence to the very end, in order to make your hope sure.
>
> HEBREWS 6:11

Michelle looked out of her office window at her employees. She knew they had been looking to her, waiting to see how she would handle herself over the past four weeks. She was tempted to throw all her energy into a new pursuit, but she also knew that she had a commitment to see this old one to its end. It was a matter of integrity. The new company would never know if she spent her time—their time now—on this new pursuit. But she would know, and her employees would know. That's not how she wanted to do business. With a forced smile, she sat at her desk and focused her mind on the issues of the day. When she finally handed this company over, she would do so knowing that she had done her best to the very end.

Change takes place in all of our lives. One season ends, and another begins. We may say good-bye to a job, a relationship, a town, or a dream. With each ending, we have a choice. We can either walk away without looking back and ignore the closure and attention that's needed; or we can take the time, painful as it may be, to finish well — to tie up loose ends, to say our good-byes, to work hard right to the end, and to give of ourselves freely so we can begin a new adventure, knowing we have closed out the old one with integrity.

Is there an area of your life that needs attention to-day — something that needs to be finished well? Take a moment and ask God to help you close the door. Only then will you be blessed in your new beginning.

When one door is shut, another opens.

MIGUEL DE CERVANTES

HELP!

What was I thinking? Kristy thought as she stood in the middle of the church's commercial kitchen and turned around slowly. As the hubbub from the fellowship hall continued, the dirty dishes were piling up on every possible surface.

"I've already loaded the dishwasher once," her friend Carol said. "You can wash pots and pans until the cycle is finished. I'm sorry I have to desert you, but I really have to run."

Kristy felt overwhelmed, but she didn't want to complain. "No problem . . . really."

By the time the dishes were washed, dried, and put away, she and another woman were the only ones left in the kitchen. Mrs. Carson, an elderly woman who had been in their church forever, had taken pity on her and stayed to help.

"I don't know what I would have done if you hadn't stayed," Kristy said, smiling. She hugged her plump helper.

"Oh, this was nothing, dear!" Mrs. Carson said. "You

Let us not get tired of doing what is right, for after a while we will reap a harvest of blessing if we don't get discouraged and give up.

GALATIANS 6:9 TLB

should have been here before we had a dishwasher."

"I can't imagine."

"Of course, people were a little different back then. We all pitched in, and the work was done in no time. Now people are so busy; they're stretched to the limit. I suppose even you have to get up and go to work in the morning."

"Yes, ma'am."

"Well, you might not get many thank-yous from other people, but God sees your heart. He's pleased with you. Now let's get you home."

When you feel like no one else cares about doing what's right or pitching in to help, remember, God cares, and He will extend His grace to you.

For grace is given not because we have
done good works, but in order that we
may be able to do them.

SAINT AUGUSTINE OF HIPPO

PASS IT ON

In truth I perceive that God shows no partiality.

ACTS 10:34 NKJV

Through the years, kitchens have played a major role in Connie's life. When she was growing up, she lived on a farm surrounded by aunts, uncles, cousins, siblings, her mother, and her grandmother. She often remembered the hot summer days when the kitchen would be steamy because they were canning. Canning was a family affair. The men raised and harvested the crops; the children peeled, chopped, and prepared the produce; and the women cooked and did the actual canning. There was much lively discussion over recipes, techniques, and timing.

At some point during the day, Grandma would sneak Connie under the table and give her a taste of whatever was being canned. (She especially liked Grandma's pickled peaches.) Grandma would warn her to keep this their special secret. In fact, it was such a secret that Connie didn't find out until a few years ago that Grandma did this for all her cousins and siblings. That discovery didn't make them love Grandma any less. It made them all feel special.

Because of it, Connie always thought she was Grandma's favorite grandchild, and that knowledge had sustained her through many rough times. When she found out that everyone in her generation thought they were Grandma's favorite grandchild, it didn't diminish that special feeling. She didn't feel betrayed. She was awed by the love that Grandma gave to the whole family. Her grandmother became the model for the kind of person she wanted to be.

God is the same way. He loves each one of us as if we were the only person in the universe. We are individually and personally His own special children.

Now as Connie makes gingerbread men with her own grandchildren, she passes along to them the knowledge that each and every one of them is as special to her as they are to God, and she prays that they will someday pass it along to their own grandchildren—maybe even in the kitchen.

A Grandma knows the art of giving from
the heart.

E. C. RAYBURN

KITCHEN FRIENDS

How wonderful to see the goodness of God in my own kitchen! Jennifer thought as she browsed through her cookbook collection. He had provided abundantly for her and her family. Not only did they enjoy a variety of good foods, He had provided the kitchen and all its tools. He also had given her a talent she loved, cooking, and it was not just for herself, but for the enjoyment of her family and friends.

And God had given her the joy of discovery. Jennifer loved finding new ideas and recipes. While reading about food, she had discovered that the "old" nutritional values found in the book of Leviticus in the Bible are just as valid today as when God gave them to the Israelites when they came out of Egypt.

Share with God's people who are in need. Practice hospitality.

ROMANS 12:13

People loved to visit together around her kitchen table, probably because her yellow kitchen was bright and cheerful. They seemed to feel warm and accepted there. Over the years, her table had been the scene of a lot of sharing, delight, heartbreak, good times, games, food, and plenty of fellowship. On holidays, everyone trooped in and out of the kitchen, helping with the cooking, visiting, carrying cups of coffee or other drinks to family members, stirring, laughing, and bumping into each other.

One day, Jennifer saw a holiday commercial on television in which the woman was thankful for instant food so she could get out of the kitchen and spend more time with her family. She wondered why the woman's family didn't spend more time in the kitchen with her!

Even the family members who are not in Jennifer's kitchen at the moment are still participating in what is going on. She remembered one year when her mother was making gravy at the stove while her dad, who was sitting in the living room, kept calling instructions to her and answering her questions as to amounts of ingredients and stirring time.

Is your kitchen the kind of place where everyone feels comfortable and welcome? If not, how can you make it a spot that binds you closer to your family, friends, and God? It might be as easy as planning a pizza night or baking chocolate chip cookies together. Give it a try!

Happy is the house that shelters a friend.

RALPH WALDO EMERSON

THE REAL STUFF

Veronica placed the cake on the dining-room table. Wiping the sweat from her brow, she surveyed the scene before her. Streamers lined the ceiling, cups and plates were set out, and the warm glow of candles added the perfect touch. It was her Henry's seventieth birthday; she was determined that it be an extra special occasion.

> O Lord, you have searched me and you know me.
>
> PSALM 139:1

The guests began arriving, and Veronica directed them to the living room. It didn't work. It never seemed to work. Every time she had a gathering, people always seemed to gravitate toward the kitchen. She sighed as she pushed through the crowd to finish her preparations. Everyone was laughing, talking, and seemed right at home. Veronica stopped for a moment as a friend warmly embraced her. She couldn't stay angry.

The kitchen was the heartbeat of her home. It didn't matter what room she intended for people to go to, they always ended up in the kitchen, gathered around the table like family. She smiled. The mess didn't matter; the fancy decorations in the other rooms didn't matter. It was the heart that people wanted—the real stuff—the comfort of home.

God is the same way in His love for us. He doesn't need the fancy stuff. He doesn't require hanging out with us at our formal best. He loves who we are—the messy, comfortable heartbeat of our very beings. That's who He wants to spend time with, who He's drawn to, who He created. You don't have to fake it with God. Just let Him love you.

————————————————

You are not accepted by God because you deserve to be, or because you have worked hard for him; but because Jesus died for you.

COLIN URQUHART

A LOAF OF BREAD

Janice looked at the recipe book and then back to the mixing bowl. She kept up a constant stream of conversation with herself as she added each ingredient. "Okay . . . okay, Janice. One egg, one cup of flour, one banana . . . mix well. Don't mess this up, just take it slow. How hard can this be? Not hard, not hard at all! They'll love it!" She paused. "What if they don't love it? What if they think I'm a horrid cook, out to poison the neighborhood?" She shook the thoughts away, determined to press on.

> Love your neighbor as yourself.
>
> LEVITICUS 19:18

Later that evening, Janice wrapped her slightly misshapen loaves of banana bread in plastic wrap. After a deep breath, she walked to her neighbor's home and rang the doorbell. An older man answered and greeted her in surprise. "Hi."

"Oh, hi! Yes . . . um . . . I'm your neighbor, Janice. I wanted to bring you this loaf of banana bread." Her cheeks reddened. "Well, basically, because I thought you might like it . . . not that I'm a great cook or anything. I mean, it IS actually edible, it's just that I'm not exactly what you would call a professional."

His grin interrupted her. "Really?" He reached out a tentative hand and took a loaf. "That was so very kind of you. I love banana bread." Janice wanted to grab it back. He loved it? Oh, no! What if it was terrible? What if she turned him away from fruit breads for life?

He seemed to read her frantic thoughts. "I'm sure it's wonderful, Janice. Thank you. You made my evening . . . just with your thoughtfulness."

Janice smiled, relieved.

It's risky to give of ourselves! Sometimes we hardly know how to share friendship and love with our neighbors. What we do, though, isn't really important. It's the thought, the time, the interest we show that make a difference in those around us. Take a moment and think of the neighbors on either side of your home. What can you do this very day to let them know you care?

The way in which something is given is worth more than the gift itself.

FRENCH PROVERB

GET UNDERSTANDING

Sometimes it seems life is lived backwards! When we are young and have only a limited perspective, we have to make the huge decisions of life that will shape the rest of our years. But we can—and are wise to—learn from those who have gained insight from life's experiences.

In a sociological study, fifty people over the age of ninety-five were asked the question: If you could live your life over again, what would you do differently? Three general responses emerged from the questionnaire.

- I would reflect more.

- I would risk more.

- I would do more things that would live on after I am dead.[25]

An elderly woman wrote this about how she would live her life if she had it to live over again:

I'd make more mistakes next time; I'd relax; I would limber up; I would be sillier than I have been this trip; I would take fewer things seriously; I would take more chances; I would climb more mountains and swim more rivers; I would eat more ice cream and less beans; I would perhaps have more actual troubles, but I'd have fewer imaginary ones.

You see, I'm one of those people who lives sensibly and sanely hour after hour, day after day. Oh, I've had my moments, and if I had it to do over again, I'd have more of them. In fact, I'd try to do nothing else, just moments, one after the other instead of living so many years ahead of time.[26]

Listen and learn! Life cannot be all work and no play, and yet you want your life to be meaningful to God, to your loved ones who follow you, and to yourself.

Reflect on your life tonight. Ask God to show you the true meaning of your existence, what you are to accomplish—and how to have fun along the way!

Knowledge comes, but wisdom lingers.

ALFRED, LORD TENNYSON

HIS PROMISE OF PEACE

A woman who grew up on a large farm in Pennsylvania fondly remembers some special times with her father. Because the growing and harvest seasons were pretty much over from November through March, she recalls thinking that her father set aside that time each year just to be with her:

Be still, and know that I am God.

PSALM 46:10

During the winter months, Dad didn't have to work as hard and long as he did the rest of the year. In fact, it seemed like there were some times when he didn't work at all as far as I could tell.

During those long winter months, he had a habit of sitting by the fire. He never refused my bid to climb up on his lap and he rewarded my effort by holding me close for hours at a time. Often, he would read to me, or invite me to read a story to him. Sometimes I would fall asleep as we talked about all the things that are important to dads and little girls. Other times, we didn't talk at all. We just gazed at the fire and enjoyed the warmth of our closeness. Oh, how I treasured those intimate moments.

As I grew, I thought it odd that other kids dreaded the "indoor" days of winter. For me they meant the incredible pleasure of having my father very nearly all to myself.[27]

Just as winter is God's season of rest for the earth, we sometimes experience "winter" in our spiritual lives. The world may seem a cold place. Like children who dread "indoor days," we can feel stifled and penned in by these spiritual winters.

If you are going through a dry, wintry time, why not snuggle close to the Heavenly Father tonight, and listen to His gentle voice? The love and comfort He wants to give you will surely warm your heart!

Peace is always beautiful.

WALT WHITMAN

CRADLED

A number of years ago, two young women boarded a ferry to cross the English Channel from England to France. About halfway through their five-hour journey, the ferry hit rough waters, and a crew member later told them they were experiencing one of the roughest seas of the year! The ferry tossed about rather violently on the waves, to the point where even the seasoned crew felt ill.

At the time the ferry hit rough water, the two women were eating a light lunch in the back of the boat. They quickly put their sandwiches away. One woman lamented, "It's hard to eat while you're riding on the back of a bucking bronco!"

> Now will I arise, saith the Lord; I will set him in safety from him that puffeth at him.
>
> PSALM 12:5 KJV

When it became apparent that the pitching of the boat was not going to abate, one of the women decided to return to her assigned seat in the middle of the ferry. She soon fell sound asleep and experienced no more seasickness. Toward the end of the trip, after the ferry had moved into calmer waters off the coast of France, the other woman joined her. "That was awful," she exclaimed. "I was nauseated for two hours!"

"I'm sorry to hear that," said the second woman, almost ashamed to admit that she hadn't suffered as her friend had.

"Weren't you sick?" the first woman asked in amazement.

"No," her friend admitted. "Here at our seats I must have been at the fulcrum of the boat's motion. I could see the front and back of the boat were moving up and down violently, but here, the motion was relatively calm. I simply imagined myself being rocked in the arms of God, and I fell asleep."

All around you today, life may have been unsettling and stormy. It may seem like your entire life is bouncing about on rough waters. But when you return to the "Center" of your life, the Lord, He will set you in safety. Let Him rock you gently to sleep, and trust Him to bring you through the rough waters tomorrow.

All I have seen teaches me to trust the creator for all I have not seen.

RALPH WALDO EMERSON

UNIQUELY FASHIONED

As you lie in bed tonight, stretch your limbs in all directions and then relax for a moment to ponder the fact that your body has been fearfully and wonderfully made. The word fearfully in this context is like the word of supreme quality that has been popular among teens in recent years, Awesome!

When you stop to think about all the intricate details involved in the normal functioning of your body—which is just one creation among countless species and organisms on the planet—you must conclude, "The Designer of this piece of work had a marvelous plan."

Listen to your heartbeat. Flex your fingers and toes. As you do these things, keep in mind the following facts:

• No one else among all humanity has your exact fingerprints, handprints, or footprints.

• No one else has your voiceprint.

• No one else has your genetic code—the exact positioning of the many genes that define your physical characteristics.

I will praise thee; for I am fearfully and wonderfully made: marvelous are thy works; and that my soul knoweth right well.

PSALM 139:14 KJV

Furthermore, nobody else has your exact history in time and space. Nobody else has gone where you've gone, done what you've done, said what you've said, or created what you've created. You are truly a one-of-a-kind masterpiece.

The Lord knows precisely how you were made and why you were made. When something in your life goes amiss, He knows how to fix it. When you err or stray from His commandments, He knows how to woo you back and work even the worst tragedies and mistakes for your good when you repent.

You have been uniquely fashioned for a specific purpose on the earth. He has a "design" for your life. It is His own imprint, His own mark. Make a resolution in these night hours to be true to what the Lord has made you to be and to become.

In order to be irreplaceable one must
always be different.

GABRIELLE COCO CHANEL

AGE IS AN ATTITUDE

Helen Keller was once asked how she would approach old age. She responded:

Age seems to be only another physical handicap, and it excites no dread in me. Once I had a dear friend of eighty, who impressed upon me the fact that he enjoyed life more than he had done at twenty-five. "Never count how many years you have, as the French say," he would insist, "but how many interests you have. Do not stale your days by taking for granted the people about you, or the things which make up your environment, and you will ever abide in a realm of fadeless beauty."

It is as natural for me, certainly, to believe that the richest harvest of happiness comes with age as that true sight and hearing are within, not without. Confidently I climb the broad stairway that love and faith have built to heights where I shall "attain to a boundless reach of sky."[28]

The poem "How Old Are You?" reinforces this idea that outlook is what determines our age:

QUIET MOMENTS WITH GOD for WOMEN

Age is a quality of mind:
If you have left your dream behind,
If hope is cold,
If you no longer look ahead,
If your ambition fires are dead —
Then you are old.
But if from life you take the best,
And if in life you keep the jest,
If love you hold;
No matter how the years go by,
No matter how the birthdays fly,
You are not old.[29]

Years before we reach what we would call "old age" we determine whether that time will be a gracious and pleasant time or a time when we rehearse life's hurts with bitterness. The attitudes with which we invest our days now will characterize the days of our senior years.

It's not how old you are but how you are
old.

UNKNOWN

THE SUNSET DECISION

Jenny Lind, known as "The Swedish Nightingale," won worldwide success as a talented She sang for heads of state in many nations and thrilled hundreds of thousands of people in an era when all performances were live.

Not only did her fame grow, but her fortune increased as well. Yet at the height of her career, at a time when her voice was at its peak, she left the stage and never returned.

She must have missed the fame, the money, and the applause of thousands—or so her fans surmised—but Jenny Lind was content to live in quiet seclusion with her husband.

Once an English friend went to visit her. He found her on the beach with a Bible on her knee. As he approached, he saw that her attention was fixed upon a magnificent sunset.

They talked of old days and former acquaintances, and eventually the conversation turned to her new life. "How is it that you came to abandon the stage at the apex

> If serving the Lord seems undesirable to you, then choose for yourselves this day whom you will serve . . . but as for me and my household, we will serve the Lord.
>
> JOSHUA 24:15

of your career?" he asked.

Jenny offered a quiet answer that reflected her peace of heart: "When every day, it made me think less of this (laying a finger on the Bible) and nothing at all of that (pointing to the sunset), what else could I do?"

Has a busy, successful life robbed you of some of the most precious gifts of God? Next time you miss a sunset or prayer time because of a crowded schedule, remember Jenny's priorities.

Nothing in life is as precious as your relationship with your Heavenly Father, and then your relationships with family members and friends. Ultimate fulfillment comes not in career or money, but in relationship with God and others.

If we fully comprehend the brevity of
life, our greatest desire would be to please
God and to serve one another.

JAMES C. DOBSON

RUNNING ON EMPTY

Some years ago, a research physician made an extensive study of the amount of oxygen a person needs throughout the day. He was able to demonstrate that average workers breathe thirty ounces of oxygen during a day's work, but they use thirty-one. At the close of the day they are one ounce short, and their bodies are tired.

> There remains, then, a sabbath-rest for the people of God; for anyone who enters God's rest also rests from his own work, just as God did from his.
>
> HEBREWS 4:9-10

They go to sleep and breathe more oxygen than they use to sleep, so in the morning they have regained five-sixths of the ounce they were short. The night's rest does not fully balance the day's work!

By the seventh day, they are six-sixths or one whole ounce in debt again. They must rest an entire day to replenish their bodies' oxygen requirements.

Further, he demonstrated that replenishing an entire ounce of oxygen requires thirty to thirty-six hours (one twenty-four-hour day plus the preceding and following nights) when part of the resting is done while one is awake and moving about.

Over time, failure to replenish the oxygen supply results in the actual death of cells and, eventually, the premature death of the person.

A person is restored as long as he or she takes the

seventh day as a day of rest.[30]

Sound familiar? The God who created us not only invites us to rest, but He created our bodies in such a fashion that they demand rest.

Most people think that "keeping the Sabbath" is solely an act of devotion to God. But in turning your attention to Him, He can offer you true rest and replenishment in every area of your life — spirit, soul, and body. He is not only our daily Strength, He is our Source of rest, recreation, and replenishment.

I feel as if God had, by giving the
sabbath, given fifty-two springs in every
year.

SAMUEL TAYLOR COLERIDGE

DISCRETIONARY TIME

Modern time-saving appliances and devices give us the opportunity to make choices about how to use our time. We can spend less time doing things we don't enjoy in order to have more time to do the things we do enjoy. But what is it we enjoy doing?

> In all your getting, get understanding.
>
> PROVERBS 4:7
> NKJV

Twenty-year-old college student Amy Wu wrote about her aunt who "tends to her house as if it were her child." The house is spotlessly clean and usually smells of home-cooked meals. Roses from the garden are artfully arranged in beautiful, vases. Her aunt could afford a housekeeper, but she truly enjoys doing her own housework.

Amy went on, "I'm a failure at housework. I've chosen to be inept and unlearned at what my aunt has spent so much time perfecting. At thirteen, I avoided domestic chores as my contribution to the women's movement. Up to now, I've thought there were more important things to do."

But those "more important things" didn't turn out to be all that important. She explained, "It isn't as if we're using the time we save for worthwhile pursuits . . . Most of my friends spend the extra minutes watching TV, listening to stereos, shopping, hanging out, chatting on the phone, or snoozing."

One day she decided to make a meal for her family. While the dinner was cooking, she wrote a letter to her cousin. Then she made a chocolate cake to celebrate her sister's birthday. It was a success: "That night I grinned as my father and sister dug into the pasta, then the cake, licking their lips in appreciation. It had been a long time since I'd felt so proud. A week later my cousin called and thanked me for my letter, the first handwritten correspondence she'd received in two years."

She concluded, "Sure, my generation has all the technological advances at our fingertips. We're computer-savvy, and we have more time. But what are we really saving it for? In the end, we may lose more than we've gained by forgetting the important things in life."[31]

Choose to spend your discretionary time wisely, caring for family and growing closer to the Lord. In all your getting, get understanding!

The great rule of moral conduct is, next
to God, to respect time.

JOHANN KASPAR LAVATER

RESTING IN THE LORD

There is a story about an English steamer that was wrecked on a rocky coast many years ago. Twelve women set out into the dark stormy waters in a lifeboat, and the boisterous sea immediately carried them away from the wreckage. Having no oars, they were at the mercy of the wind and the waves. They spent a fearful night being tossed about by the raging tempest.

> He who dwells in the shelter of the most high will rest in the shadow of the almighty.
>
> PSALM 91:1

They probably would have lost all hope if it had not been for the spiritual stamina of one of the ladies, who was well known for her work in sacred oratorios. Calmly she prayed aloud for divine protection. Then, urging her companions to put their trust in the Lord, she encouraged them by singing hymns of comfort.

Throughout the dark hours her voice rang out across the water. Early the next morning a small craft came searching for survivors. The man at the helm would have missed the women in the fog if he had not heard a woman singing the selection from Elijah, "Oh, rest in the Lord, wait patiently for Him!" Steering in the direction of her strong voice, he soon spotted the drifting lifeboat. While many others were lost that night, these trusting few were rescued.

Have you ever had a long sleepless night when the

trials and "storms" of the day refused to leave you? Have you found yourself unable to sleep because of worries about what tomorrow may bring? Perhaps you have felt you were adrift in an ocean of responsibilities with no rescue in sight.

Instead of laying there awash in worry, frustration, fear, or anger, try singing hymns of faith—either aloud or silently—in your mind. As you turn your thoughts to the true Rescuer, you are likely to find yourself relaxing in His arms and drifting off to sweet sleep.

God washes the eyes by tears until they
can behold the invisible land where tears
shall come no more.

HENRY WARD BEECHER

ULTIMATE WORTH

You are
Christ's, and
Christ is
God's.

1 CORINTHIANS
3:23 NKJV

"Going . . . going . . . gone!" The bidding was over, and the auctioneer's gavel fell. The winning bid for a rocking chair that had been valued between $3,000 and $5,000 was $453,500.

This had been the case through the duration of the auction. A used automobile valued between $18,000 and $22,000 was sold for $79,500. A set of green tumblers valued at $500 sold for $38,000. A necklace valued at $500 to $700 went for $211,500. For four days articles of common, ordinary value were sold for wildly inflated prices. Why? The items auctioned were from the estate of Jacqueline Kennedy Onassis.

How do we assess value? How do we determine what is valuable to us?

As in the sale of the items of the Kennedy estate, some things are valuable solely because of the one to whom they belong. Paul wrote to the Corinthians, "You were bought at a price" (1 Corinthians 6:20 NKJV).

Peter wrote, "You were not redeemed with corruptible things, like silver or gold, . . . but with the precious blood of Christ" (1 Peter 1:18-19 NKJV). The price Paul and Peter are talking about was the price for our sin, paid by Jesus Christ in His death on the cross.

We may inflate a person's worth because of their financial status, their influence, or their potential to benefit us; or we may say a person has no value because they have few assets or cannot help us. But the Scriptures tell us that when we were still sinners, Jesus Christ died for us. (See Romans 5:8.) When we had no value and were even opposed to God, He paid the price to redeem our lives.

Every individual on the face of the earth is someone for whom Jesus died. Because of the great price of redemption, all people, regardless of their financial worth, are of great importance.

Whenever you feel depressed and worthless, meditate on this: Your value is determined by God. He loved and valued you so much, He sent His Son to die so you could become His child. Never doubt your importance and worth!

All I could never be, all men ignored in me—this, I was worth to God.

ROBERT BROWNING

RITUALS

T he word "ritual" is derived from the word, "rite," which means "a ceremonial or formal, solemn act, observance, or procedure in accordance with prescribed rule or custom."[32] A ritual refers to a system of rites—in other words, doing the same thing in the same way, every time. Rituals are common customs unique to an era or group of people.

A heart at peace gives life to the body.

PROVERBS 14:30

The word rite originally had a religious connotation. The best-known rites of the church, in the past as well as the present, have been baptism, communion, joining the church, marriage, and burial. These rites give a comforting continuity when the meanings remain alive and cherished.

For example, when a new convert and the congregation understand that water baptism is a outward statement of what has already taken place inwardly—the "old man" has died with Jesus Christ (going under the water) and is raised with Jesus Christ (coming out of the water)—the baptismal service becomes a powerful time of worship.

On a more mundane level, in present day society a ritual can be anything performed on a regular basis. It can now refer to something as simple as brushing our teeth. Whether we realize it or not, we all have rituals. The things we do to prepare for work in the morning and the things we do when we get home each night are rituals that give order, meaning, and security to our lives.

Just like religious rituals, our daily rituals can bring us peace and comfort or leave us frustrated and lifeless. Our daily routine should include rituals which balance and enhance our lives spiritually, mentally, emotionally, socially, professionally, and physically.

A devotional time before bed touches every area. Praying purifies the heart, reading the Word of God renews the mind, receiving more of the Heavenly Father's unconditional love evokes feelings of serenity, communing with the Lord gives us a sense of belonging and guides us in our work—and all these things put the body in a relaxed, peaceful state.

When I am with God my fear is gone in the great quiet of God. My troubles are life pebbles on the road, my joys are like the everlasting hills.

WALTER RAUSCHENBUSCH

RESTORATION

In a remote Swiss village stood a beautiful church. It was known as the Mountain Valley Cathedral. The church was not only beautiful to look at, with its high pillars and magnificent stained glass windows, but it also had the most incredible pipe organ in the entire region. People would come from miles away — even from far-off lands — to hear the lovely tones of this organ.

One day a problem arose. The columns were still there, the windows still dazzled with the sunlight, but an eerie silence enveloped the valley. The area no longer echoed with the glorious fine-tuned music of the pipe organ.

Musicians and experts from around the world tried to repair the instrument. Every time a new person would try to fix it, the villagers were subjected to sounds of disharmony — awful noises that seemed to pollute the air.

One day an old man appeared at the church door. He spoke with the sexton, and after a time the sexton reluctantly agreed to let the old man try his hand at repairing the organ. For two days the old man worked in almost

Those who hope in the Lord will renew their strength. They will soar on wings like eagles; they will run and not grow weary, they will walk and not be faint.

ISAIAH 40:31

total silence. The sexton was getting a bit nervous.

Then on the third day, at precisely high noon, the valley once again was filled with glorious music. Farmers dropped their plows, merchants closed their stores, everyone in town stopped what they were doing and headed for the Cathedral. Even the bushes and trees of the mountaintops seemed to respond as the glorious music echoed from ridge to ridge.

After the old man finished playing, a brave soul asked him how he could have restored the magnificent instrument when the world's experts could not. The old man merely said, "It was I who built this organ fifty years ago. I created it—and now I have restored it."

God created you, and He knows exactly what you need to live your life to the fullest. As your Creator, He can restore you at the end of a draining day—so you can play beautiful music tomorrow!

He who plants a tree, plants a hope.

LUCY LARCOM

FINISHING STRONG

The Gospel accounts of Matthew, Mark, and Luke tell us that Jesus ended His earthly life and ministry by crying with a loud voice, obviously from a great surge of energy. Luke tells us further that in His cry, Jesus commended His spirit to the Lord, giving His all to the Father.

What a wonderful example of how we might end our work each day!

First, we need to "finish strong." In the afternoon, we often must refocus and double our efforts. Those who work in offices often find their most productive hour is the last hour of the day, when everyone else has gone home and the phone has stopped ringing. Those who work at home also tend to experience an end-of- the-day urgency to get things done before shifting to more relaxed hours.

We are wise to pray as we enter the home stretch of a day, "Father, give me Your strength and energy to bring to a conclusion what I have started. Help me now to go the extra mile."

Second, we need to commend our work to the Lord. As we finish our work, we need to say, "Thank You, Lord, for the energy, health, and creativity to do what I have done today. Now, I turn over all rights to what I have done to You. I trust You to winnow out what is worthless and to cause that which is worthy to last and benefit others. I give it all to You."

To finish strong and commend our work to the Lord requires humility. We must recognize that the Lord is the Source of all our ability and power to accomplish and succeed.

As you pause this afternoon, choose to finish your day well, and then give what you have done to the Lord.

Religion is no more possible without prayer than poetry without language or music without atmosphere.

JAMES MARTINEAU

POWER STEERING

Few things in life make us feel as powerful as sitting behind the steering wheel of a car. Realizing the vehicle weighs two tons and is capable of traveling up to one hundred miles per hour, we have a tendency to feel almost invincible—which is a good feeling after a long, hard day at work.

Unfortunately, this heady sensation often results in dangerous or rude behavior, such as changing lanes without signaling, driving too fast, tailgating, failing to yield to merging traffic, running red lights or stop signs, flashing headlights, and blaring horns. When we give in to the urge to do just one of these things, reasoning, "It won't hurt to do it this once," or "I'm in a hurry," or "Everyone else does it," we become part of a problem instead of part of a solution.

> Whatever is born of God overcomes the world; and this is the victory that has overcome the world— our faith.
>
> 1 JOHN 5:4
> NASB

How should you act when you're in the driver's seat at the end of your workday, headed for home? Pop some uplifting music, such as praise songs, into the tape deck, or listen to the soothing sounds of a classical station. Say a quick prayer for safety before you start the engine, and decide you'll be a friendly, courteous driver and not a road hazard. Use this time for personal rejoicing over the work you've just completed.

What do you do when other drivers seem to be going out of their way to make your drive time a "drive-you-crazy" time? Resist the urge to scream, shake your fist, or respond in kind to whatever the offending drivers do. Instead, say a prayer for them, smile, and wave. Let them wonder if they know you from somewhere!

Have faith in God to turn any problem into a blessing. You'll have a much nicer evening when you finally arrive home!

———————————————

Beware in your prayer, above everything,
of limiting God, not only by unbelief, but
by fancying that you know what he can
do.

ANDREW MURRAY

TAKE TIME FOR BEAUTY

One thing I have desired of the Lord, that will I seek: . . . to behold the beauty of the Lord.

PSALM 27:4
NKJV

"Keep a place in life for beauty," says English preacher Leslie Weatherhead. "He who keeps a little place in his life for beauty will find that it does something for him and in him, and that something is a process that goes on when the beauty is no longer before his eyes and ears, like a seed growing secretly in the dark. God, by a secret ministry, can turn the sight of a snowflake into hope and the sight of the dawn into courage."[33]

Beauty feeds our souls like food nourishes our bodies. Beauty points us to the transcendent, takes us beyond our finiteness and opens our hearts to that which is greater and larger than ourselves. There is something about great beauty that brings us into the awesome presence of the infinite and the eternal.

In reflecting on his priorities, a prominent British scientist said he would give more time to the enjoyment of things that are beautiful. He said:

> *If I had my life to live over again, I would have made a rule to read some poetry and listen to some music at least once a week; for perhaps the part of my brain now atrophied would have thus been kept active through use. The loss of these tastes is a loss of happiness, and may*

possibly be injurious to the intellect, and more probably to the moral character, by enfeebling the emotional part of our nature.[34]

We sometimes need to be reminded to slow down enough to find beauty in those things we hurry by each day. Let's take time for beauty. Make a date with yourself to stroll through an art gallery, visit a beautiful church, or linger in a park or garden.

If there simply is not time, then remember the beautiful places captured in memories — moments of sheer joy or a mental "snapshot" of a majestic, snowcapped mountain or moonlit night.

Let God use the beauty He created to awaken in you the desire for more of Him.

———————————————

At cool of day, with God I walk my garden's grateful shade; I hear his voice among the trees and I am not afraid.

UNKNOWN

UNDER WATER

Teatime is a wonderful time to regroup, rethink, and refresh. It comes at the time of day when we are a bit frayed from the day's activities, but the activities are not yet at an end. Unfortunately, not all of us can stop for a real tea break, but without this break, the remaining tasks may threaten to take us "under."

> He knoweth the way that I take: when he hath tried me, I shall come forth as gold.
>
> JOB 23:10 KJV

As the shadows of the day grow longer, our tempers can grow short. Drawing on the refreshing power of the Holy Spirit, however, will get us to the end of a stressful day. We can gain renewed patience, a fresh sense of humor, and a new surge of creativity and insight by enlisting the aid of the Spirit's ministry within us. Frequently it's during those late afternoon hours when we most need His extra help.

Jewelers claim one of the surest tests for diamonds is the underwater test. "An imitation diamond is never so brilliant as a genuine stone. If your eye is not experienced to detect the difference, a simple test is to place the stone under water. The imitation diamond is practically extinguished, while a genuine diamond sparkles even under water and is distinctly visible. If a genuine stone is placed beside an imitation one under water, the contrast will be apparent to the least experienced eye."

That is how it should be with Christians when their heads are "under water" at the end of the day. The power of the Holy Spirit should so sparkle within them, refreshing and renewing them in spite of the day's harassments, that it should be easy for the average person to tell there is something genuinely different about their lives.

Ask the Holy Spirit to impart His power and presence to you today, in this very hour. Pray for Him to help you in the ways you need Him most—to make you shine like a diamond under water!

In the morning, prayer is the key that
opens to us the treasures of God's
mercies and blessings; in the evening, it is
the key that shuts us up under his
protection and safeguard.

UNKNOWN

IS ANYONE OUT THERE?

One of the biggest complaints some of us have about life today is the feeling that we have more interaction with machines than we do with people. Ever since computers became essential business tools and televisions became the entertainment centers in most homes, it's been getting harder to have meaningful human contact in our daily lives. It's even more difficult to find people who will go out of their way to do something kind for a person they've never met.

> "Let your light shine before men, that they may see your good deeds and praise your Father in heaven."
>
> MATTHEW 5:16

When a uniform factory in the Midwest closed its doors for what was presumably the last time, one of its customers did just that. As the factory workers were facing certain unemployment in their small town, this gentleman decided to buy and reopen the plant. Needless to say, the workers were amazed, pleased, and disbelieving.

The man, a native Midwesterner who owned several uniform shops on the West Coast, had come into a large fortune. He believed that if your cup was full and running over, you should share your blessings with others. When he tried to place an order and found out that the uniform factory had gone out of business, he decided to put his philosophy into action.

The customer bought the factory and started putting

people back to work. He provided his employees with their first health plan, jazzed up the uniform styles to make them more attractive to buyers, began replacing outdated machinery, and made other improvements to the plant.[35]

Do you have to be rich to bring a ray of sunshine into someone's life? Not at all! Sometimes money is involved in making a meaningful change, but it's really the person who signs the check and his or her desire to do something good that is behind it.

No matter how much or how little we have, we can each do something to make someone else's path a little smoother.

Give to the world the best you have, and
the best will come back to you.

UNKNOWN

CIRCADIAN MEETINGS

A business consultant once advised executives to follow this pattern for scheduling their meetings and appointments:

• Have breakfast meetings to set agendas, give assignments, and introduce new projects.

• Have lunch meetings to negotiate deals, give advice to key staff members, and discuss midcourse corrections.

• Have afternoon meetings to interview prospective employees, clients, or vendors, to return phone calls; and to resolve personnel issues.

From this consultant's perspective, morning hours are best spent in task activities, midday hours in problem-solving, and afternoon hours in people-intensive activities. The reason has little to do with management and much to do with biology. Our "circadian rhythms" seem to put us at a high-energy time in the morning and a low-energy time in the afternoon. Meeting with people requires less energy than attention to task and detail.

> To everything there is a season, a time for every purpose under heaven.
>
> ECCLESIASTES 3:1 NKJV

This afternoon, perhaps you can meet a friend or invite colleagues into your office for a bit of refreshment and conversation. Schedule relationship-building meetings in the afternoon. Take time out for a brief end-of-the-day conversation with a secretary or another person who works under your supervision. Allow time for light conversation and share about personal matters—such as the antics of a toddler or accomplishments of a teen in the family.

Jesus no doubt spent full days in ministry, preaching, teaching, and healing those who flocked to Him. But at the close of His ministry-intensive hours, Jesus spent time with his friends. We are not only wise to follow His example—it appears to be the way we were created!

Hast thou a friend, as heart may wish at will? Then use him so, to have his friendship still. Wouldst have a friend, wouldst know what friend is best? Have God thy friend, who passeth all the rest.

THOMAS TUSSER

PLAYTIME!

Do you remember how you felt when you were a child and the final bell of the school day sounded? Freedom! Time to play!

For most children, the time immediately following school is set aside for the following things:

• Unstructured fun — no more assignments to be completed in a specific class period.

• Noise and activity — no more restrictions to sit still and be quiet.

• Friendships — no more working on your own to read a book or complete an assignment.

• Games — workbooks are left behind, and homework is yet to come.

What ever happened to those good ol' days? you may wonder. Perhaps it is time to recapture them.

Build in a little playtime at the end of your workday. Let it be unstructured. Allow yourself to be a little noisy. Move about, and flex those tired muscles. Spend a little time with friends. Play a game — perhaps handball with a colleague, a set of tennis with a friend, or a game of hopscotch with your child.

We all know the saying, "All work and no play makes

for a very dull day." Believe it! Not only will the day be dull, but you are likely to be dull as well.

The Lord made you with a capacity for fun, an ability to smile and laugh, a desire to kick up your heels and frolic a bit, and a need for freedom of motion. He created the world for you to enjoy — and to enjoy it with Him!

The Scriptures say that the Lord "delights" in us. Could it be that the Lord delights in what delights us? Could it be that the Lord desires to have someone with whom to have complete fellowship, including someone with whom to laugh, play, and relax?

Could it be? Why not find out today!

Human fellowship can go to great lengths, but not all the way. Fellowship with God can go to all lengths.

OSWALD CHAMBERS

THE TEA CART

Be kind to one another, tenderhearted.

EPHESIANS 4:32
NKJV

A number of years ago, a corporation experimented with the recommendation of one of its vice-presidents. At three o'clock each afternoon for a month, a tea cart pushed by a maid in uniform mysteriously appeared on the executive floor. The cart was laden with fine china and linen napkins, as well as silver urns and trays of simple but elegant sweets. Executives and their secretaries and administrative assistants were invited to come out of their offices and from behind their desks to select a flavor of tea and a sweet treat from the cart.

Moments of pleasantry and conversation followed naturally. In many cases, people who had worked on the executive floor for years met their colleagues for the first time or became better acquainted with them.

After a month, the president of the company conducted an informal poll among those who had enjoyed a "month of tea." He discovered that, without exception, each person reported a new air of civility on the floor. Many employees commented on how much they had enjoyed the tea break and on how they felt this service had increased morale.

Encouraged by such positive results, the president ordered a "tea cart" service for each of the floors in the corporate building. The same benefits were noted by all of the employees. Shortly thereafter, the service company noted an increase in customer satisfaction, and in its wake a significant rise in profit. Although no one was so bold as to say a tea cart impacted profit . . . could that be the case?

A kind word, a kind deed, a kind attitude—they all speak volumes. They impact the way we think of ourselves and others, which impacts the way we work. The apostle Paul certainly knew this to be true when he advised, "Be of good comfort, be of one mind, live in peace; and the God of love and peace will be with you" (2 Corinthians 13:11 NKJV).

Make a rule, and pray to God to help you keep it. Never, if possible, to lie down at night without being able to say: "I have made one human being at least a bit wiser, or a little happier, or at least a little better this day."

CHARLES KINGSLEY

OPPOSITES BALANCED

M uch of our life seems to be suspended between opposites. We grow up learning to
label things as good or bad, hurtful or
helpful, naughty or nice. People are kind or mean. The
thermostat can be adjusted to avoid extremes of heat and
cold. We look forward to the changing of seasons from
summer to winter. Time is divided by day and night.

Not only are these opposites helpful to us in defining
or "bordering" our lives, but they can also help us release
stress.

Very often people who are engaged in physical, mus-
cle-intensive work all day choose a mental activity with
which to relax and unwind. Those who have idea-inten-
sive jobs often enjoy relaxing with hobbies that make use
of their hands, such as woodcarving or needlework.
Those in sterile, well-ordered environments look forward
to going home to weed their gardens.

Structured tasks and routines are good relaxation for
those involved in the creative arts. The musician runs
home to the computer. The surgeon delights in growing
orchids in a hothouse. The factory worker enjoys cross-
word puzzles. The executive unwinds in the kitchen,

The day is yours, the night also is yours; you
have prepared the light and the sun. You
have set all the borders of the Earth; you
have made summer and winter.

PSALM 74:16-17 NKJV

preparing gourmet meals.

The Lord created us for this rhythm of opposites. God told Noah as he and his family left the ark that Noah would experience "Seedtime and harvest, Cold and heat, Winter and summer, And day and night Shall not cease" (Genesis 8:22 NKJV). Human beings were set in a world of opposites.

When you feel stressed out at day's end, try engaging in an activity that is opposite in nature to the work you have been doing. If you have been using your mind, turn to an activity that is physical. If you have been exerting physical energy, turn to an activity that is mental.

Let the pendulum swing back to rest in a central location!

Nothing is at last sacred but the integrity
of your own mind.

RALPH WALDO EMERSON

A LITTLE CEREMONY, PLEASE

Afternoon tea at London's Ritz Hotel is described as the last delicious morsel of Edwardian London. Helen Simpson offers this description in The London Ritz Book of Afternoon Tea:

> *In the elegantly columned Palm Court, the light is kind, the cakes are frivolous and the tempo is calm, confident and leisurely. Takers of tea perch on rose-colored Louis XVI chairs at marble tables, sipping their steaming cups of tea . . . There are no clocks, and although it is just possible to glimpse the flash of Piccadilly's taxis and buses if you look hard in the direction of the doors, a strange sense of taking a holiday from time heightens the pleasure of taking tea here. People look more beautiful than they do in real life due to the flattering lighting. Here is one of the few places outside church . . . where a woman may wear a hat and feel entirely at ease . . . Those approaching the Palm Court clad in such garments as jeans, shorts or sneakers will be reluctantly turned away and no one is admitted without a reservation. The dark tea leaves are steeping in boiling water when brought to the table with a selection of tiny finger sandwiches, scones and cakes.[36]*

Why all that fuss over a cup of tea and a snack?

Because the "ceremony" of drinking afternoon tea provides more refreshment than the food and drink alone can deliver. It requires the participants to cease all other activities for a short period of time, take in a little sustenance, and give attention to others who are sharing the repast. It is an opportunity for one to put down whatever knotty problems have been occupying the day thus far and take up lighter issues for a few minutes. The body gets refreshment and rest, and the mind gets a little vacation.

Teatime also provides a natural opportunity for the spirit to be refreshed. Taking tea alone gives one the chance to reflect on the ups and downs of the day in quiet prayer, receiving fuel to move confidently through the rest of the day.

If you are "taking tea" with a friend or friends, why not share one thing that God has done for each of you. Praise at teatime gives a new meaning to the phrase "high tea!"

Praise is more than singing, it's the saint reflecting the life of Christ.

UNKNOWN

ON A CLEAR DAY

Ask any person who exercises on a regular basis, and he or she will tell you that the benefits of a good workout go far beyond the physical. Many people end their workday with a trip to the gym. Doing so helps them to clear their head of the day's frustrations, gives them more energy to face the evening ahead, calms them down, and improves their mood. It is also a complete departure from sitting at a desk all day.

While any exercise can be helpful, research has shown that where you exercise can make a big difference in the benefits derived from a workout session. A psychologist at an East Coast university tracked hormonal and mood changes in a group of runners who participated in three different jogs:

- Outdoors
- Indoors, on a treadmill, while listening to "sounds of nature" tapes
- Indoors, on a treadmill, while listening to tapes of

> You will go out with joy, and be led forth with peace; the mountains and the hills will break forth into shouts of joy before you, and all the trees of the field will clap their hands.
>
> ISAIAH 55:12 NASB

their own heartbeats

Can you guess which jog proved to be the most beneficial? The outdoor jog. Levels of the positive mood hormones adrenaline and noradrenaline were up, while the levels of the stress hormone cortisol were down in those who had exercised outside.

It seems environment really matters. Whether you're exercising or just taking a few moments to relax with a cup of tea, where you do it can be nearly as important as why and how you do it. Find a delightful, stimulating spot for your getaway, and make the most of your break.

As children, we often asked our neighborhood friends, "Can you come out and play?" It's still a good question to ask!

Those who do not find time for exercise
will have to find time for illness.

UNKNOWN

SIMPLE PLEASURES

There are many ways to enjoy teatime—formal, casual, business, cream teas, Christmas tea, tea served in a mug, tea presented in a fine china cup, a picnic tea outdoors in the country, a cozy, snuggled-up-beside-the-fireplace tea for two, an elegant tea on the lawn, or an hour of culinary delight in a stylish tea room.

Briton Aubrey Franklin was appointed "Tea Ambassador" to America by the Tea Council of the U.S.A. to instruct Americans in the proper use of tea. He recollects his memories of childhood teatimes in England:

When I was a young lad, teatime was that special hour for sharing stories and having a giggle or two with my family. These everyday gatherings, enhanced by the ritual of teatime, helped us to feel united. To be able to chat about the humorous and of times tremulous events of the day was not only cathartic, but enabled us to know and enjoy each other. This is what is needed today, a time set aside for the specific purpose of sharing not only tea and its delicious accompaniments, but love. . . . Instead of friends and families tuning out by immediately switching on the telly, start tuning in to one another again. Teatime is the perfect time and is a most delightfully exhilarating habit.[37]

Life's simple pleasures are those we most frequently ignore — often in pursuit of greater and grander schemes of happiness.

However you choose to do it, try to set aside some casual time to spend with a friend or loved one for no other reason than to relax, enjoy a laugh, rekindle intimacy, help soothe each other's jangled nerves, or just to let your minds wander together among uncharted dreams.

Friendships multiply joys and divide griefs.

UNKNOWN

ACCESSIBILITY

The end of a workday is a time when you may find it very pleasant and beneficial to make yourself a little more accessible to other people. If you have had a "closed-door, nose-to-the-grindstone" attitude all day, now may be the time to open the door. If you've been on the phone for what seems like hours, now may be the time to wander the halls and have a brief face-to-face conversation with a colleague or someone you supervise. If you have felt bogged down with paperwork or glued to a computer screen, now may be the time to walk to the cafeteria and get an energizing snack. Invite someone to go with you or meet you there for a few conversation. If you have been indoors with children or house chores, it might be time to call a neighborhood friend and go for a walk.

Robert Fulghum has written: "The grass is not, in fact, always greener on the other side of the fence. Fences have nothing to do with it. The grass is greenest where it is watered."

Every day, regardless of our environment or situation, we need to have human contact and communication. God built this need into us, and from the story of God's relationship with Adam and Eve in the Garden of Eden, we can assume that God enjoyed a late-in-the-day stroll with His creation—a time of sharing lives, not simply working together on tasks.

Share with others in a heart-to-heart way. Listen with open ears to the feelings a person may be expressing, even more closely than you listen to the details of their story. Be willing to help carry their burdens and rejoice at their victories. Allow yourself to be vulnerable to others in return — revealing your own wounds, concerns, worries, frustrations, hopes, dreams, and desires. Accessibility is the first key to a genuine relationship.

Of all the heavenly gifts that mortal men
commend, what trusty treasure in the
world can countervail a friend?

NICHOLAS GRIMALD

BREWING GOOD RELATIONSHIPS

Most tea-drinkers would never consider tossing a tea bag in the nearest cup of hot water as the proper way to make a cup of tea. When one wants the best pot of tea, there are several rules for brewing that will assure the tea is a treat for the palate.

> A word fitly spoken is like apples of gold in settings of silver.
>
> PROVERBS 25:11 NKJV

Always choose teas whose basic flavors are pleasing to you or your guests. If they are loose teas, don't be afraid to do a little blending, measuring one teaspoon per cup plus one teaspoon per pot. Let the tea steep for several minutes, but don't boil tea leaves. If you do, bitter tannins will emerge.

Like brewing tea, forming good relationships takes time and attention to be satisfying. Here are ten ways to show the love of Jesus to others — guaranteed to bring out the best "flavor" of each person:

1. Speak to people. There is nothing as nice as a cheerful word of greeting.

2. Smile at people. It takes seventy-two muscles to frown, fourteen to smile.

3. Call people by name. The sweetest music is the sound of one's own name.

4. Be friendly and helpful.

5.   Be cordial. Speak and act as if everything you do is a pleasure.

6.   Be genuinely interested in people. You can like everybody if you try.

7.   Be generous with praise — cautious with criticism.

8.   Be considerate of the feelings of others. It will be appreciated.

9.   Be thoughtful of the opinions of others.

10. Be alert to give service. What counts most in life is what we do for others.[38]

These things take time, but like the time spent perfecting that pot of tea, it is well worth the extra effort.

The greatest thing a man can do for his heavenly Father is to be kind to some of his other children.

HENRY DRUMMOND

READ THE BOOK

Two women who were having lunch together in an elegant gourmet restaurant decided to end their repast with a cup of tea. The tea arrived and was poured into exquisite china teacups, but after taking the first sip one woman complained to the waiter. "Sir, this tastes like benzene. Are you sure it's tea?"

The waiter replied, "Oh, yes, it must be. The coffee tastes like turpentine."

If you are serving a pot of tea, you will have good results with this recipe:

1. Rinse out the teakettle and start with fresh, cold tap water. Never boil anything but water in your teakettle.

2. Bring the water to its first rolling boil. Never over-boil! Over-boiling takes the oxygen out of the water, which in turn creates a flat beverage.

3. Take the teapot to the teakettle and rinse out the pot with the boiling water from the kettle. Never take the kettle to the teapot, as you lose one degree of heat per second. Water for tea must be 212 degrees.

4. Use one teabag or teaspoon of loose tea per cup. Leaves enter the warm teapot and the infusion begins

when the leaf opens.

5. Pour hot water gently over the leaves. Be careful not to bruise the leaves.

6. Allow the tea to brew for three to five minutes, according to the blend of tea and how strong you like it.[39]

Following the instructions of connoisseurs can help us make a good cup of tea. The same is true in living a good life!

The Bible is God's instruction book: "All Scripture is given by inspiration of God, and is profitable for doctrine, for reproof, for correction, for instruction in righteousness" (2 Timothy 3:16 NKJV). We are wise to follow its instructions!

A bit of the book in the morning, to order my onward way. A bit of the book in the evening, to hallow the end of the day.

MARGARET SANGSTER

TEMPEST IN A TEAPOT

Have you had a tempest in a teapot kind of day? Perhaps you are disoriented by a bad night's sleep, distressed over the phone call from your child's teacher, or pressured by the impending review by your boss. On days like that it's easy to erupt into a storm over the least trifling matter. Times like that become opportunities to say yes to God.

> All the promises of God in him are yes, and in him amen, to the glory of God through us.
>
> 2 CORINTHIANS 1:20 NKJV

In her book Diamonds in the Dust, Joni Eareckson Tada asks, "Do you remember when you said 'yes' to Jesus? How long ago was it? A few months, maybe years? I said 'yes' to the Lord in November 1964 when I was a teenager. But I also said 'yes' to Him just the other day."

Tada describes a day when she had a quarrel with her husband Ken. To escape the situation, she went with a friend to the shopping mall, where she burst out in sobs of self-pity. She said, "I couldn't hide my face in a tissue, and my wheelchair was too big for me to escape behind several clothes racks. All I could do was sit there, cry, and stare at the mannequins with the plastic smiles."

Trying to recover from waves of sobs, she said aloud what she had said many times before, "Yes, Jesus, I choose you. I don't choose self-pity or resentment. I say 'yes' to you!"

With her face still wet with tears, she felt her heart fill with peace. She said, "Nothing about my husband had changed. Shoppers on the other side of the store still picked through the racks . . . teenagers still ambled by, giggling and eating popcorn . . . but everything was different because of my peaceful heart. Because I said 'yes' to Jesus."[40]

We may not even know the full extent of what troubles us, but we can give our frustrations and unsettled emotions to God. We can pray to Him, "Lord, I don't understand this situation, but I know I want Your peace and Your grace to change me in the midst of this storm in my life. Thank You for caring enough about me that You gave me the desire to say yes to You. Amen."

It is a pity that our tears on account of
our troubles should so blind our eyes that
we should not see our mercies.

JOHN FLAVEL

FEAR NOT

D riving across the country by herself, a young woman recorded this experience:

> Those of steadfast mind you keep in peace—in peace because they trust in you.
>
> ISAIAH 26:3 NRSV

I was on the second leg of a three-leg journey, and all I wanted to do was find a motel, park the car, remove a day's accumulation of traveling dust from my weary body, and fall into bed for a good eight hours. But I couldn't stop, because I hadn't met my mileage goal for the day. I was still more than two hours from Tucumcari, New Mexico, and tired though I was, I was also bound and determined to get as close to the Texas border as I could.

What I hadn't reckoned on was bad weather. California and Arizona had been sunny and warm, and I wrongly assumed that New Mexico in late March would hold no unpleasant surprises.

The sun was sinking fast behind me, and soon disappeared altogether. On cross-country trips, I prefer not to drive at night – especially on unfamiliar roads – but I had a goal to meet that day, and so I pushed on.

A quarter hour or so after sunset, I saw precipitation gliding past the glow of my headlights. Rain, I thought. But no, it was snow. Soon it was coming down fast and furiously at a slant, directly into my windshield, having a kaleidoscopic effect.

Panic took hold. There were few cars on the interstate, no lights along the route, no parking lots to pull into and wait it out.

It wasn't the fiery furnace, but it was an ordeal I needed to work my way through. And since I couldn't see where I was going as well as I would have liked, I had to put all my faith and trust in Someone who could. I had to somehow relax in the midst of this dark, wintry valley and rely on light from another Source.

I made it safely to my destination that night – not because of superior driving skills or dumb luck, but because I learned a long time ago Who it is who really keeps my car on the road.

Fear knocked at the door. Faith answered.

No one was there.

INSCRIPTION OVER MANTEL OF HINDS'
HEAD HOTEL, ENGLAND

BEST FRIENDS

A student working on her doctoral thesis spent a year on a reservation in the Southwest, living with a group of Navajo Indians. As the student did her research, she became part of a Native American family. She slept in their home, ate their food, worked with them, and generally lived their lifestyle.

The grandmother in the family did not speak English, yet she and the student were able to form a close bond of friendship. They spent much time together, forging a relationship that was meaningful to each one, yet difficult to explain to anyone else. The two shared experiences together even though they could not talk with each other. In spite of the language difference, they developed a closeness of mutual understanding and affection.

> You were called into the fellowship of his son, Jesus Christ our Lord.
>
> 1 CORINTHIANS 1:9 NRSV

Over the months each one of them worked to learn phrases in the other one's language. The student learned some Navajo phrases, and the old grandmother picked up some English words.

When the year ended, it was time for the student to return to campus to write her thesis. The tribe held a going-away celebration in honor of her stay and their friendship. The celebration was a sad occasion because the young woman had become close to the entire village;

she would miss them, and they would miss her.

As the student climbed into her pickup truck to leave, her dear friend, the old grandmother, came to say good-bye. With tears flowing down her cheeks, the grandmother put her hands on either side of the student's face. She looked directly into the young woman's eyes and said in her newly learned words: "I like me best when I'm with you."

Good friends are the ones around whom we "like ourselves best" because they have a way of bringing out the best in us. Jesus is that kind of Friend to us. We can share all of our life with Him, and He still accepts us with His great love. He will bring out the best in us so we can say to Him, "I like me best when I'm with You."

What is a friend? A single soul dwelling in two bodies.

ARISTOTLE

A HEART FOR ART

Do good, O
Lord, to
those who
are good,
and to those
who are
upright in
their hearts.

PSALM 125:4
NASB

Whether you prefer coffee or tea, there's something special about going to a coffee house or tearoom—places specifically created for sitting down with a warm mug and basking in a soothing ambiance. And if you happen to find yourself at Cafe Lam in Hanoi some afternoon, you can also enjoy gazing at a small portion of the owner's priceless art collection.

Nguyen Van Lam began selling coffee from a cart in 1950. Several years later, he bought a building near an art school. Many of his customers were struggling art students who could barely afford to put food in their stomachs, much less buy art supplies. Lam, an impassioned art lover, loaned them money so they could practice their craft.

Several of the artists—who later became quite famous—repaid Lam's generosity with paintings, prints, and drawings. Over the years, his collection grew to more than a thousand pieces of art. Only a small portion of the collection is displayed in the cafe, but it covers almost every square inch of wall space.

Lam's extensive collection is a precious treasure. To protect the art during the war, he even went to the extent of storing the art in an air-raid shelter. These days, he hopes to turn his building into a museum to permanently display his collection for future generations to enjoy.

Lam loves artists as much as he loves art. He admires their generous spirits, their ability to find beauty in everything, and the way they pour themselves into their work without demanding something back.

To casual passersby, the building that houses Cafe Lam is a dilapidated, nothing-to-look-at edifice. But for those willing to come inside, there is a cup of good coffee and beauty as far as the eye can see.[41]

Time with Jesus can be time spent in a lovely art gallery, where He shows you all the colors and patterns of your life. Just as Lam cared for the struggling artists, Jesus cares for you. He is your Comforter, Friend, Protector, and the Source of all creativity and beauty. Thank Him today for His love for you.

God's love for us is proclaimed with each
sunrise.

UNKNOWN

REDIRECTED ANGER

A Salvation Army officer stationed in New Zealand tells of an old Maori woman who won the name Warrior Brown for her fighting ability when she was drunk or enraged. After her conversion to Christianity, she was asked to give her testimony at an open-air meeting. One of her old enemies took the opportunity to loudly make fun of her. He ended his harangue by throwing a large potato at her, which hit her with a nasty blow.

> A gentle answer turns away wrath, but a harsh word stirs up anger.
>
> PROVERBS 15:1

The crowd grew deadly silent. A week earlier, the cowardly insulter would have needed to sprint into hiding to salvage his teeth. But what a different response they witnessed that night!

Warrior picked up the potato without a word and put it in her pocket. No more was heard of the incident until the harvest festival came around, when she appeared with a little sack of potatoes to share. She explained she had cut up and planted the potato and was now presenting it to the Lord as part of her increase.

Warrior had learned how to live in peace with her neighbors and yet be a strong spiritual "warrior" for the Lord's cause. What a beautiful example of taking the ill people do and turning it into praise for the Father in Heaven!

President Lincoln was once taken to task for his amiable attitude toward his enemies. "Why do you try to make friends of them?" asked an associate. "You are a powerful man. You should try to destroy them."

"Am I not destroying my enemies," Lincoln gently replied, "when I make them my friends?"

What might you do today to show kindness to an enemy? When you treat your enemy as a friend, and your enemy responds in friendship, you have turned your enemy into your friend!

The heart benevolent and kind the most
resembles God.

ROBERT BURNS

OPEN THE DOOR

A nurse on duty in a pediatric ward often gave the children an opportunity to listen to their own hearts with her stethoscope. One day she put the stethoscope into a little boy's ears. She asked him, "Can you hear that? What do you suppose that is?"

The little boy frowned a moment, caught up in the wonder of this strange tapping inside his chest. Then he broke into a grin and responded, "Is that Jesus knocking?"

Another story is told of a group of students who went to visit a great religious teacher. The wise teacher asked the young scholars a seemingly obvious question: "Where is the dwelling place of God?"

The students laughed among themselves and replied, "What a thing to ask! Is not the whole world full of His glory?"

The learned old man smiled and replied, "God dwells wherever people let Him in."

The little boy listening to his heart through the stethoscope seemed to have more wisdom than the group of

Behold, I stand at the door, and knock; if any man hear my voice, and open the door, I will come in to him, and will sup with him, and he with me.

REVELATION 3:20 KJV

students. With his innocent, trusting faith, he had no problem believing that Jesus was knocking on his heart's door.

Imagine your life to be a house of many rooms. Each room represents a different aspect of your life. Some of the rooms are messed up; others are clean and tidy. The doors that are locked represent areas where you have not invited Jesus to enter.

Like the little boy, when we hear Jesus knocking at the closed doors of our life, it is up to us to open the door and let Him in. Even those rooms that are dark and frightening are filled with light and understanding when Jesus enters.

Lord, make my life a window for your light to shine through and a mirror to reflect your love to all I meet. Amen.

ROBERT HAROLD SCHULLER

DOWNSHIFTING

A few years ago, an automobile manufacturer used the slogan, "We are driven." The automaker might have been talking about most of the human race! We are a people on a mission: work nonstop, master the learning curve, and achieve as much as possible as fast as we can.

> He who dwells in the shelter of the most high will rest in the shadow of the almighty.
>
> PSALM 91:1

For all our enthusiasm and energy, however, we start out strong in the morning and then fall prey to gloomy weather, dark moods, or weariness toward teatime. We feel driven to finish what's in front of us, but we don't have the stamina to go on. That's when we have to resort to Plan B.

Plan B says that if you don't want to leave your office yet, but you are burned out on weightier matters, you have to do something lighter. Select a job-related task that doesn't require a lot of brainpower.

Write a letter, organize a file, type some notes, gather reference materials, return a phone call, or write memory-joggers on your calendar for upcoming meetings. Give your eyes a break from the computer screen and close them for a couple of minutes.

In *The Spirit of Discipline*, Bishop Francis Paget writes:

When it is dull and cold and weary weather with us, when the light is hidden, and the mists are thick, and the sleet begins to fall, still we may get on with the work which can be done as well in the dark days as in the bright; work which otherwise will have to be hurried through in the sunshine, taking up its happiest and most fruitful hours. Very often, I think, the plainer work is the best way of getting back into the light and warmth . . . Through humbly and simply doing what we can, we retrieve the power of doing what we would.

Until your concentration level is back to normal, switch to automatic pilot and glide for a little while!

Inside myself is a place where I live all alone, and that's where you renew your springs that never dry up.

PEARL S. BUCK

HIS WAY

A Danish author tells the story of an old peasant who made an unusual request of his son as he lay dying. He asked his son to go into the best room of the house every day and sit there alone for half an hour. The son agreed to the strange request and promised his father he would do what he had been asked.

> In quietness and confidence shall be your strength.
>
> ISAIAH 30:15
> NKJV

After his father's death, the son kept faithful to his promise. He did this unusual thing—spending a half hour alone each day. At first the time of quiet and solitude was uncomfortable. He became restless and anxious for the time to end. But over the weeks, that half hour of solitude grew into a cherished and even transforming habit. The son looked forward to this brief quiet period each day and even began to thrive on it. He began to experience deep and calming changes within himself.[42]

Are you willing to be alone for fifteen or thirty minutes each day, preferably when your mind is not overtired? Are you willing to take an adventure of expectant faith, not looking for a predefined experience or not seeking an emotional high, but asking Jesus to come to you in His own way?

With your body relaxed and comfortable, and looking only to Jesus, your heart will be turned to Him in adoration. From this experience, you are likely to have a greater desire to obey Him. People who devote time to be alone with the Lord find a renewed reservoir of personal strength and quiet confidence.

The world desperately needs people who are trying out Jesus' way of life and have an ever-deepening experience of Him. They are looking for peace and joy that lasts, and those qualities only show up in the lives of believers who allow Jesus to reign in their hearts.

Spend some peaceful moments alone with the Lord today and watch the peace and joy in your heart grow and spill over into the lives of others.

A happy life consists of tranquility of mind.

MARCUS TULLIUS CICERO

AN OPEN DOOR

One warm summer afternoon, a woman was attending the baptism of her grandniece in a great old stone church in the English countryside. The massive doors of the church were flung wide to allow the warm sunshine into the chilly stone structure.

As she sat enjoying the ritual, a small bird flew in through the open doors. Full of fear, it flew backward and forward near the ceiling, vainly looking for a way out into the sunshine. Seeing the light coming through the dark stained glass windows, it flew to one, then the next, and finally back toward the ceiling. It continued flying about in this way for several minutes, quickly exhausting its strength in frenzied panic. The woman watched the bird with concern and frustration. How foolish it was not to fly back out the same door through which it had entered!

Nearly ready to fall to the floor, the bird made a final lunge for one of the large rafters. Realizing it was in no immediate danger, it hopped a little on the beam, turned around, and suddenly saw the open door. Without hesitation it flew out into the sunshine, loudly singing a joyful song as it went.

The bird had captivated the woman's imagination. Suddenly she realized that she was like the bird. She had flitted about, trying to live a "good" life of noble works without recognizing that the door of salvation had been open to her all the time. She suddenly understood that to avoid flying errantly into places that offered no hope of eternal life, she need only stop flapping and be still in the Lord's presence. From that vantage point, she could better see the door of grace that He had prepared for her.

During your teatime break today, let your spirit fly up to a high place and sit with the Lord. He will show you how to fly out of your current problems.

The deepest wishes of the heart find
expression in secret prayer.

GEORGE E. REES

TOOLS OF THE TRADE

We see it as we walk along an ocean shore, where steep cliffs meet with the rise and fall of the tides. The splashing of sand and rock-laden waves have cut away at the towering sea cliffs. Day after day, night after night, the continual lapping of the ocean water silently undercuts the stone walls. Then in one sudden blow the entire structure can shift and fall thunderously into the sea. On a daily basis, the wear and tear of water on sea cliffs is imperceptible, yet we know that every wave hitting the rock is washing away some of its hard surface.

> We are his workmanship.
>
> EPHESIANS 2:10 RSV

We see the same shaping influence in another aspect of nature—trees that grow at the timberline, a harsh, remote setting. The extra resins that flow in the trees, as a result of the severe winds and snowstorms at the timberline, produce a grain of wood that has a rare and desirable texture.

Such wood is sought by violin makers because it produces instruments of the finest quality and resonance. Fierce storms, the short growing season, and whipping winds combine to yield some of the choicest wood in all the world.[43]

When we are subjected to the endless wear and tear of life, we develop faults and cracks in our lives. In God's hands, however, those stresses and changes become His tools for shaping our lives for His purpose. As our lives are yielded to and shaped by Him, He creates within us the ability to resonate His presence.

The varied and often difficult experiences of life, given to God, are how He transforms each individual into something beautiful. The Holy Spirit can work wonders on the rough edges of our stubborn wills and hard hearts, conforming them to His own will.

Commit your life to the Lord again this afternoon. Trust Him to take all that happens to you—both good and bad—and make you stronger and wiser, using you in His great plan.

Whate'er we leave to God, God does and blesses us.

HENRY DAVID THOREAU

"WE INTERRUPT
YOUR LIFE . . ."

Living longer is supposed to be a good thing. None of us wants to die "before our time." We want to see children and grandchildren and sometimes great-grandchildren grow up. We want to travel, enjoy the homes we worked so hard to build, and do all those things we dreamed of before and after retirement.

> I will sing to the Lord all my life; I will sing praise to my God as long as I live.
>
> PSALM 104:33

Life doesn't always turn out the way we planned. Yes, we might be living longer, but so are our parents. And oftentimes, parents have major health concerns that require constant care.

As children we were the cared for, but somehow we have become the caregivers. We had our life compartmentalized, but the model has to be broken because Mom or Dad has doctor appointments, therapy sessions, or activities to attend at a senior center—and we are the chauffeurs.

Mom needs groceries and someone to cook her meals. Dad's house needs to be cleaned, and the lawn needs mowing. Mom is lonely and needs someone to sit and talk to her for a couple of hours. Dad needs help buying clothes. An adult child's life can disappear in the process of caregiving.

Take positive steps if you find yourself in the role of caregiver for elderly parents. It helps to have a friend you can visit with from time to time — someone who isn't too close to the situation. You need the perspective he or she can give. It also helps to find a support group of people who have learned how to care for their parents with wisdom and joy.

Start each day by saying, "I'll do my best today," and avoid criticizing yourself for not doing everything perfectly. Take care of yourself! You can't help anyone if you get sick due to lack of rest, poor nutrition, or stress.

Above all, make your caregiving an act of love and not obligation. Ask the Lord for His grace and His peace to surround you, and whisper prayers to Him throughout the day.

Prayer serves as as edge and border to
preserve the web of life from unraveling.

ROBERT HALL

POWER NAPS

H ave you ever considered trading in your afternoon break for a quick nap?

Medical students are usually adept at taking power naps. They fall asleep immediately upon lying down, sleep for fifteen to twenty minutes, and then awake refreshed. Researchers have discovered these short naps are actually more beneficial than longer mid-day naps. The body relaxes, but does not fall into a "deep sleep," which can cause grogginess and disorientation.

Only one thing is required for people to sleep this quickly and benefit fully from a power nap—the ability to "turn off the mind." We quiet our minds by not thinking about all that remains to be done, worrying about all that might happen, or fretting over events in the past.

Power nappers are experts at inducing a form of inner peace that comes from knowing all will be well with the world while they check out for a few minutes. What they believe with their minds actually helps their bodies relax.

When King Hezekiah told the people the Lord was with them and would fight their battles, they rested upon his words. His words gave them inner peace, confidence,

With him is an arm of flesh; but with us is the Lord our God to help us, and to fight our battles. And the people rested themselves upon the words of Hezekiah King of Judah.

2 CHRONICLES 32:8 KJV

and a rest for their souls. We can take those same words to heart today.

The Lord is with us also, to help us and to fight our battles. These simple lyrics from a Bible-school chorus say it well:

You worry and you wonder how you're gonna get it done,
From the rising of the moon 'til the setting of the sun.
Plenty to do when your rest is through,
Let Him have the world for a turn or two.

Take time to rest today.

There will be plenty to do when you wake up . . . so sleep on for a few minutes. Rest and be thankful.

WILLIAM WORDSWORTH

THIRST-QUENCHERS

W ater is essential to the survival of plants, animals, and people. The life processes of an organism depend on its cells having moisture. A tree, for example, may be 80 percent sap, which is primarily water. Sap contains minerals, carbohydrates, vitamins, and proteins, which circulate through the tree's vascular system to feed all parts of the tree.

Whosoever will, let him take the water of life freely.

REVELATION 22:17 KJV

The amount of the water supply in an area determines whether it is a desert or a forest. It determines whether a tree is shriveled and stunted or towering and majestic. Water comes to trees through dew, clouds, mists, fog, summer rains, and winter snows. Trees also take in water through their roots, which tap into springs, streams, or rivers.

A tree does not hoard moisture for itself, but after the water travels through the framework of the tree, it is given off into the surrounding air. The moisture, along with the oxygen expelled into the air, give the forest a fresh fragrance.

The spiritual lesson we learn from nature is that it is nearly impossible to be a blessing to others when we are grossly undernourished ourselves. Like the tree, we must be well-watered with God's Word and His Spirit to bring a sweet fragrance to those around us.

If you are feeling empty and dry this afternoon, go

to the watering hole of God's Word and take a long, re-freshing drink. Feel His truth permeate every cell of your being and rejuvenate love, peace, and joy in your heart. It won't be long until you're looking for ways to help someone else!

What I kept, I lost. What I spent, I had.
What I gave, I have.

PERSIAN PROVERB

DECISION-FREE HOURS

Sing to him,
sing psalms
to him; talk
of his
wondrous
works. Glory
in his holy
name.

PSALMS 105:2-3
NKJV

Kate declared the hour between three and four o'clock in the afternoon a decision-free hour in her office! She announced this to her staff in a lighthearted way, but she was secretly intent upon making it a reality.

As the supervisor of nearly thirty people, all of whom had access to her because of her open-door policy and easy style of management, Kate was asked to make decisions incessantly. This left little time for creative interaction or easy conversation with her staff members and colleagues.

At first, Kate's staff found the habit hard to break. "What can we say if we aren't asking you a question?" her secretary finally asked in a tentative voice.

"Tell me something!" Kate suggested. "Anything! Tell me something funny that has happened in the office today, or something that is happening in the lives of the staff or their family members. Clue me in to a new idea, or give me a creative suggestion. Just don't ask me to make a decision or to respond in any way except to ask a question of my own or make a casual comment."

Over time, Kate found that people were quick to stop by her office between three and four o'clock just to say "hi," to share a bit of news, or to compliment a fellow employee. Her decision-free hour became the most positive hour in the day, and the information she received actually helped her become a better manager—and make wiser decisions.

Could it be that the Lord might also enjoy some decision-free, problem-free, no-answer-required-from-Me hours with us, His children and coworkers in the world? Could it be that He'd enjoy hearing prayers in which we simply tell Him what is happening, what we find funny or interesting about our lives, and what delights us or gives us joy? Could it be that He'd enjoy hearing a good joke from our lips, rather than a string of incessant petitions?

It just might be.

He prays well who is so absorbed with
God that he does not know he is praying.

SAINT FRANCIS DE SALES

INVISIBLE WORK

Trees have specific seasons for dormancy—a time when they appear to be inactive and not growing. This season of rest comes immediately prior to a season of rapid and accelerated growth. During dormancy, the cells and tissues within the tree are being repaired and built up. This activity is invisible to the eye. The tree is quietly preparing for the vigor of spring.

Dormancy is one of the most important periods in the life cycle of the tree. It is how a tree becomes fit for the later demands of adding new wood to its structure and bearing its fruit.

> Faith is the assurance of things hoped for, the conviction of things not seen.
>
> HEBREWS 11:1
> NRSV

The benefits of dormancy apply to people as well. There is a mistaken notion that to be effective we must always be active. But people also have seasons in their lives when God is preparing them for what lies ahead.

Not knowing the future ourselves, we often have to come to a deep trust in God during times when nothing seems to be happening in our lives. Inactivity must not be equated with non-productivity—God is at work behind the scenes!

It takes patience and humility to get through a time of dormancy. Most of us desire to be productive at all times so we can "get ahead" in our lives. We need to recognize there are times when, unbeknownst to us, God has to work in our hearts to prepare us for our destiny.

We need to humble ourselves before Him and realize we didn't create ourselves. We can't know fully what it is we will need in our future. Dormant times call for us to wait on the Lord and trust Him to do His work in our hearts. We can rest assured He is preparing us for something great, in His timing and according to His purpose.

———————————————

It is vain to gather virtues without
humility; for the spirit of God delights to
dwell in the hearts of the humble.

ERASMUS

WRITE AWAY

As teenagers, our diaries were sacred. Woe to curious sibling or friend who dared to unlock the secrets of our lives!

Through the centuries, journals have been a precious possession to many — a place to chronicle days, record feelings, dream, complain, plot a course, and escape. Many journals have become valuable historical records, while others have served as the basis for novels or scholarly papers.

Most of us will never see our journals in print — we hope! — but we can benefit greatly from the writing process. Journaling is taking a journey through the past, the present, or the future.

Some people journal early in the morning, before the day begins, and record dreams from the night before or thoughts about the day ahead. Others journal at night, just before bed, to put the final punctuation on the day. Still others use journaling as a good excuse to take a break during the day.

One woman retreats to a favorite room late in the afternoon, before the family troops in and preparations for the evening meal begin. She sits in a comfortable chair, puts her feet up, sips a cup of tea, listens to some quiet music, and jots down thoughts in her journal. Perhaps she doesn't have the chance to do it every day, but she makes the effort to allow at least a few minutes for this stop-the-world-and-let-me-get-off indulgence.

Journaling on paper might not be suited to you. Sitting quietly and thinking about what's happened that day, and then mentally turning the frustrating parts over to God, might be your way of bringing closure to what is beyond your control. However you choose to journal, make and keep a daily appointment with the Lord for reflection. Such a time can help you unjumble your thoughts and find a suitable stride for finishing out your day.

Of all those arts in which the wise excel,

nature's chief masterpiece is writing well.

JOHN SHEFFIELD, DUKE OF
BUCKINGHAM AND NORMANDY

PARSLEY

Most of us are very familiar with parsley, those sprigs of greenery that give color to our dinner plates in restaurants. Parsley is sometimes used as a lush bedding for salad bars or as a garnish on pasta dishes and bowls of soup.

For the most part, parsley seems decorative—a pretty splash of green to brighten the culinary scene. Few of us ever eat the parsley made available to us or even think to try it. And yet that is why parsley was originally provided. It was intended to be eaten in small quantities—a few leaves consumed as the final bite from the plate. For what purpose?

Parsley is a food known to gourmets as a "palate cleanser." Eating it removes the lingering taste of foods just eaten to allow a person to experience more fully the new tastes of the next course. Parsley erases the old and makes way for the new! In fact, after a bite of parsley, most people find it difficult even to recall vividly the flavor of the foods previously eaten.

> Ye are washed, but ye are sanctified, but ye are justified in the name of the Lord Jesus, and by the spirit of our God.
>
> 1 CORINTHIANS 6:11 KJV

Another interesting fact about parsley is that if you look closely at a clump of it, you will make an amazing discovery. Like clover, parsley is a "trinity" plant. Each time a stem divides into stalks or leaves, it divides into three parts.

What a wonderful spiritual analogy we have in parsley! For surely it is our Father, Son, and Holy Spirit who cleanse us from the dust, dirt, and evil grime of the world and prepare us for the beautiful new world which Jesus called the Kingdom of Heaven. God is the One who has the capacity to remove all memories of sorrow and pain and replace them with overflowing joy and hope for the future!

Take another look at your world today. What other lessons does the Lord have for you to learn about His creative wonders? You can be assured: His entire creation points toward Him and to the glorious plan He has for you as His child.

The christian life that is joyless is a
discredit to God and a disgrace to itself.

MALTBIE D. BABCOCK

A SERVANT'S HEART

W ork is over, and you're headed home, but first there are several errands to run. When the last stop has been made and you're pulling into your driveway, you marvel once again at the all-too-common coldness of your fellow humans.

> Serve one another in love.
>
> GALATIANS 5:13

Doesn't anyone smile anymore? Can't people help me find what I'm looking for without treating me like a nuisance? Doesn't anyone apologize for making a person wait or for giving bad service?

The boss of a moving company in the Northeast has a philosophy we wish every person who serves us would emulate. Knowing what a traumatic experience it is to pack up and start a new life in a new place, he makes a point of letting his clients know he understands and cares about what they're going through. In the process, he has found it is just as easy to be kind as it is to be abrupt.

The best example we have of how to serve is the Lord Jesus. In Matthew 20:28, He told His disciples, "The Son of Man did not come to be served, but to serve." Jesus' dedication to service was evident in all He did, from teaching in the synagogues and preaching the good news, to healing the sick and performing miracles.

"When he saw the crowds," says Matthew 9:36, "he had compassion on them, because they were harassed and helpless, like sheep without a shepherd."

Isn't that the way we sometimes feel at the end of a long, hard day—harassed and helpless? Don't we want someone to treat us kindly and lead us home? What a difference it makes when people treat us well!

The law of sowing and reaping tells us that what we sow we will reap. (See Galatians 6:7.) As we become more and more servants of love and kindness to others, we will find ourselves being served with love and kindness in return.

———————————

The most acceptable service of God is
doing good to man.

BENJAMIN FRANKLIN

STUBBORN AS
AN OLD GOAT

Martin Luther had a favorite illustration he used in his sermons:

If two goats meet each other in a narrow path above a piece of water, what do they do? They cannot turn back, and they cannot pass each other; and there is not an inch of spare room. If they were to butt each other, both would fall into the water below and be drowned. What will they do, do you suppose?

As it happens, one goat will inevitably lie down while the other goat passes over it. Once the walking goat is safely on its way, the other will rise and continue on its chosen path. This way, both get where they wish to go safely.

There is a great deal of concern in today's world about allowing others to "walk all over us." But lying down to give way to another in order that both might achieve their goal is not the same as being a doormat. Nothing Jesus ever did could be considered weak and helpless. In strength and power He laid down His life for us. His example teaches us we must be willing to prostrate ourselves for others to follow His example.

When you come to impasses with people, consider what might happen if you simply yielded your pride for a moment and allowed them to

- speak their opinions,
- present their arguments,
- offer their ideas,
- suggest courses of action, or
- perhaps even make decisions.

Ask yourself, Would this change the direction I am going in my life? Will it keep anyone from Heaven?

Prostrating ourselves for the benefit of others rarely costs us anything, but it may yield great rewards, both now and for eternity!

What we have done for ourselves alone dies with us. What we have done for others and the world remains and is immortal.

ALBERT PINE

TASTE BERRIES

I n Africa there is a fruit called the "taste berry," so named because it makes everything eaten after it taste sweet and pleasant. Sour fruit, even if eaten several hours after the "taste berry," seems sweet and delicious.

Oh, that men would give thanks to the Lord for his goodness, and for his wonderful works to the children of men!

PSALM 107:8
NKJV

For Christians, gratitude is the "taste berry" that makes everything else taste sweet. When our hearts are filled with gratitude, nothing that comes our way seems unpleasant to us.

Most often we are grateful only when we are happy with our circumstances or enjoy what we have been given. However, we may need to be taught like children to say thank you for what is given to us, whether we like it or not.

A habit of giving thanks in all circumstances helps us to look beyond our immediate situation and see our lives from a higher perspective.

Sometimes the gifts given to us may not appear to be good gifts or gifts we desire. But when we learn to thank God in all things, we discover that the gifts we've received are exactly what we need.

Gratitude can also help a person who is mourning or lighten the load of a person carrying a heavy burden. It can dispel loneliness and give strength to a person in ill health.

George Herbert wrote this beautiful thank-you prayer:

Thou hast given so much to me,
Give one thing more – a grateful heart.
Not thankful when it pleases me,
As if Thy blessings had spare days,
But such a heart, whose pulse may be Thy praise.

Keep the "taste berry" of gratitude in your hearts, and all of life will be sweeter.

May silent thanks at least to God be given with a full heart; our thoughts are heard in heaven.

WILLIAM WORDSWORTH

KINDNESS BOUQUET

Not surprisingly, Kristina, a middle-aged woman who regularly practices kindness in her life, has a lot of friends. One day Peg confessed to her that she was depressed. Peg had two small children who required lots of care, and she worked part-time as a secretary to help with finances. "The hardest thing I do every day is get out of bed in the morning," Peg said. "I'm so down that I don't know what to do."

> A kind man benefits himself, but a cruel man brings trouble on himself.
>
> PROVERBS 11:17

So Kristina, in her usual manner, immediately tried to think of something, some act of kindness, to cheer her. The first thing she thought of was that her friend loved flowers. So she went in her back yard and picked an assortment of wild purple, yellow, and red flowers that gave a wonderful aroma. Next she picked a handful of wild greenery and arranged the flowers in a vase.

When Kristina delivered the flowers to Peg, her friend's brown eyes lit up. She asked, "Those are for me?"

"Yes, I picked them from my back yard. I decided you need to have some flowers so you will know I care about you."

Several days later, Kristina spotted Peg at the grocery store and asked, "How are you feeling?"

"Terrific!" Peg exclaimed with a wide grin. "You made me feel so special when you picked those flowers just for me." What she said next deeply moved and touched Kristina. "You know, I never appreciated the beautiful dandelion bouquets my children gave me, but now I do. I look at them and see that in my busy world there are so many tiny beautiful things I'd never noticed before. It's a miracle really. I'm not feeling depressed anymore."

A little act of kindness can touch someone's life forever. Preparing dinner for a tired mother, running an errand for someone, or writing a complimentary letter to a friend are a few kind acts we can incorporate into our lives. And not only do we make another person feel special, but we can feel pretty good about ourselves as well.

Little deeds of kindness, little words of love, help to make Earth happy like the heaven above.

JULIA A. FLETCHER CARNEY

CONSIDER
THE HEAVENS

A stronomers keep finding light in our dark universe.

Helen Sawyer was born in 1905, in Lowell, Massachusetts, and twenty-five years later married Canadian astronomer Frank S. Hogg. Noted for her research on what are called variable stars, Helen found more than two hundred and fifty such stars that display different degrees of brightness.

Receiving her doctorate in astronomy from Radcliffe College in 1931, Helen studied globular star clusters in the Milky Way galaxy. By studying the variable stars, she was able to determine the time required for some of these stars to change from bright light to dim light and back to bright light again. This information helped other scientists to calculate how far certain stars are from the earth.

For centuries, scientists have discovered more and more information about the light at night in our huge universe. Today scientists know that the heavens contain a mind-boggling number of stars, moons, planets, and galaxies. Most are far beyond what the naked eye can

When I consider your heavens, the work of your fingers, the moon and the stars, which you have set in place, what is man that you are mindful of him, the son of man that you care for him?

PSALM 8:3

see, and much of the light in our night sky can't even be seen with today's powerful and gigantic telescopes.

Think of the night-lights discovered during your lifetime. Then think of the night-lights still waiting to be discovered. There's no way to predict how much more future astronomers will find out about the night-lights in the universe.

Tonight, enjoy your night-light. Gaze out your windows, and count the stars. Study the moon with a telescope. Search for the Big Dipper, the Little Dipper, the North Star, and other famous night-light spots. As you enjoy light at night, you'll inevitably come to appreciate the tremendous amount of light God has provided in the universe.

Darkness is my point of view, my right to
myself. Light is God's point of view.

OSWALD CHAMBERS

ANYBODY HOME?

J ennifer, a middle-aged mother, was resting after returning home from a weekend retreat with her husband when she heard the door open.

"Hello!" a familiar young lady's voice said. "Anybody home?"

> The Lord's curse is on the house of the wicked, but he blesses the home of the righteous.
>
> PROVERBS 3:33

Both Jennifer and John hurried to the door to greet their beautiful daughter. At twenty years of age, Becky was trying to discover her place in the world. Gradually, she attempted to let go of her parents' hands and enter a world of new beginnings, a place where she would find true happiness and joy as she used the talents and abilities God had blessed her with.

Letting go of their children had been very difficult for Jennifer and John. Since Becky was the baby of the family and the only girl, it was much more difficult. Her mother had spent many sleepless nights worrying about her. At night when Jennifer would hear the door unlock, signaling Becky's safe return, she would whisper a prayer of thanks to God for placing His protective hand over her.

As the nights passed, she learned to depend on God more and more. She realized that even though she couldn't be with Becky every moment of every day, God could. Over the previous year, she had placed Becky in the hands of God, allowing Him to guide her steps. This made the nights less worry-filled and the time spent with her daughter more beautiful.

As the family was reunited, they exchanged hugs and kisses. Her parents had only been away for two nights, but to Becky it seemed like an eternity. While she wasn't home much herself, she wanted her parents to be nearby, just in case she needed them.

"I'm glad you're home," Becky said to them. "I missed you both so much."

Aren't we glad that God is always home? He never leaves our side and always offers the security that we need to live each day to its fullest. Thank you, God, for living with us in our home, the greatest earthly gift ever given.

The knowledge that we are never alone
calms the troubled sea of our lives and
speaks peace to our souls.

A. W. TOZER

ARE YOU RICH?

Amy, a young mother, longed to be rich, thinking that wealth would ease the financial strain on her self-employed husband. They lived in a moderate middle-class home, but she wanted a more expensive one.

> The sleep of a laborer is sweet, whether he eats little or much, but the abundance of a rich man permits him no sleep.
>
> ECCLESIASTES 5:12

One day Amy visited her sister in her new home, and she was impressed. A chandelier hung from the dining room ceiling. The kitchen featured every built-in appliance and gadget possible. The den boasted a large-screen television, loads of CDs, and an enviable stereo system. Amy thought, Joe and I could enjoy a home like this, too, if I went to work.

Later, after the tour of the house was over, she asked her sister what time she had to get up for work every morning. "Five-thirty," Janice replied.

Back in her own home, Amy looked at her husband with tears of gratitude in her large brown eyes. "Do you realize how rich we are?" she asked him.

"What do you mean?" Joe frowned.

"I don't have to get up early in the morning and leave our precious son at a sitter's house. I can enjoy him all day. I'm rich! I just never realized it before."

Joe laughed, grabbed Amy, hugged her, and said, "I totally agree."

In our society, it's so easy to get caught up in material things. Everywhere we look, advertisements appear before us, enticing us to buy a beautiful home, luxurious furniture, designer clothes, late-model cars, boats, motorcycles, cosmetics—you name it.

Tonight, take a look at your surroundings. See how rich you are—not with expensive, material things, but with the things that count. Do you have a pile of library books on your sofa? Or do you have nutritious foods in the cupboard? Or maybe on your refrigerator you have a priceless photo of your child. No matter what you have, take note of your blessings tonight and enjoy them.

There are two ways of being rich. One is
to have all you want; the other is to be
satisfied with what you have.

PROVERB

THE TARNISHED CUP

After hours of searching through dusty cartons in the basement and brushing aside spider webs and dust bunnies, Kelly found the box that contained the baby cup that had been her grandmother's. It was wrapped in yellowed newspaper from many years earlier, as evidenced by the dates on the paper. Kelly removed the wrapping and discovered that the cup was now blackened by tarnish. Frustrated and disappointed, she stuffed the cup back into the carton.

That night she was unable to sleep. After an hour of tossing and turning, it finally occurred to her that she was uneasy because her neglect and lack of concern had allowed the cup to deteriorate. She ran downstairs to the basement to retrieve it and brought it back up to the kitchen.

Finding some silver polish, she gently cleaned the cup until the beautiful silver was again revealed. With much work and love, the cup was restored to its original beauty.

Stop being mean, bad-tempered and angry. Quarreling, harsh words, and dislike of others should have no place in your lives. Instead, be kind to each other, tenderhearted, forgiving one another, just as God has forgiven you because you belong to Christ.

EPHESIANS 4:31-32 TLB

Often our relationships with family and friends become tarnished, and they deteriorate under layers of hurt feelings, anger, and misunderstanding. Many times the deterioration begins with a comment made in the heat of the moment or under the strain of another problem entirely. If the air isn't cleared immediately, the relationship becomes tarnished.

When we put work and love into our relationships, they can be restored. Then we rediscover the beauty that lies underneath the tarnish and realize that it has been there all along.

As you lie awake tonight, unable to sleep because you've been hurt by a loved one and you've said hurtful words or retaliated in kind, remember the teachings of Jesus and ask forgiveness for yourself and your loved one.[44]

We achieve inner health only through
forgiveness—the forgiveness not only of
others but also of ourselves.

JOSHUA LOTH LIEBMAN

LOVE'S VARIETY

There's such a variety of love in the world: the love between spouses, the love between parent and child, the love of a friend for another. In the name of love, wars have been fought, men have dueled and lost their lives, people have become alcoholics, and great achievements have been accomplished. The most unassuming individual, acting out of a heart of love, has the potential to become a hero.

However, the most unselfish love is the love Jesus has for each individual. His love is the cornerstone of our lives and the foundation of our existence as we interact with others in loving ways. Love shrivels up in isolation.

Each experience we face and every person we meet add a new dimension to the way we love. And when we open ourselves up to those we fear or dislike, we usually find new opportunities to share God's love.

> Now these three remain: faith, hope, and love. But the greatest of these is love.
>
> 1 CORINTHIANS 13:13

Love grows and thrives when it's nurtured. A man and woman who have been married for decades discover that they love each other more deeply than they could ever have imagined as newlyweds.

In your quiet time with God tonight, ask Him for the gift of love and share it with someone else tomorrow. Give your love freely, with no strings attached, just as

God gives His love to us all. Become a person of faith and hope, but most of all, become a person of love.[45]

———————————————————————

What does love look like? It has hands to help others. It has feet to hasten to the poor and needy. It has eyes to see misery and want. It has ears to hear the sighs and sorrows of men. That is what love looks like.

SAINT AUGUSTINE OF HIPPO

FOOD IN MY HOUSE

Bring the whole tithe in to the storehouse, that there may be food in my house.

MALACHI 3:10

"What? You just lost your job?" Deborah took a deep breath, then sat down quickly. She watched the laugh lines at the corners of her husband's eyes turn somber.

Although her husband had been a faithful employee of the same company for more than twenty-six years, he was let go when the company's earnings dropped. The woman watched as her husband mentally battled the onslaught of depression. "Hey," she said. "I'll take you out to eat tonight."

"Why?" he asked. "I just lost my job."

"Because I'm trying to keep you from getting depressed," she said. A grin spread across his face, and she knew she'd hit home.

Later at the restaurant as they sat across the table from each other, her husband leaned forward and whispered, "I think I'm going to be very depressed next Friday."

Deborah felt her throat clutch. "Oh," she said.

"Yeah, I think we'll have to go to Shoney's so I'll feel better," he joked.

When they got home, the first thing they did was have a time of prayer, asking specifically for God's guidance. At church, they asked people to pray. Her husband began sending out resumes and making phone calls.

Months dragged on, and depression crept into the couple's lives after they received little response from prospective employers. But when Deborah heard about Hurricane Mitch's devastation in Honduras, she immediately began gathering clothes and canned goods for the victims. Her husband stopped her, asking, "What are you doing? That's our food."

"Those people need clothes and food more than we do," she said. "I also think we should tithe on your unused vacation pay and give that to them." After writing the check, the Lord released a flood of joy in both of them. The next day, two companies called to schedule an interview.

Sometimes we have trouble giving up material things when we ourselves need them. But in His Word, God promises His children that when they are faithful to give, He will always provide abundantly for their needs.

As we give, we live.

SIDNEY GREENBERG

UNFAILING LOVE

Writer Marion Bond West wrote about "The Healing Tree" at a time when things weren't going right and she doubted her roles as wife and mother. At the time, her self-reliant older daughter was pregnant, she and her teenage daughter couldn't seem to get along, and the twin boys preferred their father.

> The Lord delights in those who fear him, who put their hope in his unfailing love.
>
> PSALM 147:11

One afternoon, she asked her husband if he wanted to go for a walk. "No," he said in a matter-of-fact way.

Disappointed, West drove to the woods and began to walk by herself. The only sounds were her own footsteps and rushing water in a stream. In the distance, she saw a lone black walnut tree. She felt like that tree—alone. At the base of the tree, she sat down. The wind churned and leaves detached from a branch, dancing in the breeze. *How easily this tree lets those leaves go!* she thought to herself. *If only I could let go as easily.*

Thinking of her husband, West picked up a branch. She prayed to release those things about him that troubled her. She tossed the stick into the water. Picking up a smaller stick, she thought, *This fragile stick is Jennifer. Please let me stop controlling my daughter's life.* She threw the stick as far as she could.

One by one, she released her children to the Lord. A

QUIET MOMENTS WITH GOD for WOMEN

larger stick represented her pregnant daughter. *Don't let me be meddlesome in her affairs*, Lord. She dropped the stick into the water.

Then she picked up twin sticks. *Don't let me press the boys into what I think they should be*. She tossed both sticks into the swirling water.

The last stick was hers. *Lord*, she prayed, *I'm not very lovable, and there's so much in me that is selfish and demanding. Do things Your way; love my family with Your unconditional love.* She dropped her stick into the stream. Immediately, she began to feel a sense of freedom, a respite from her bondage.

There's freedom in releasing our loved ones and ourselves to the Lord. When we stop clinging to past anger and disappointment, we experience the Lord's unfailing love and acceptance.[46]

To take all that we are and have and hand
it over to God may not be easy; but it can
be done, and when it is done, the world
has in it one less candidate for misery.

PAUL E. SCHERER

HEARING GOD'S VOICE

The last time Allison saw her sister, they had had a difference of opinion and decided to go their separate ways. She later learned her sister had turned her back on God.

As the years passed, Allison missed her younger sister and unsuccessfully tried to find her. For a long time, she pleaded with God to help her find Beth. Finally, she stopped begging God to answer her prayers and placed the request in His hands to do what pleased Him. The days, months, and years passed, and it seemed as though her prayers would remain unanswered.

> Be still, and know that I am God; I will be exalted among the nations, I will be exalted in the Earth.
>
> PSALM 46:10

But God had heard her prayers. Two weeks before Christmas in 1998, Allison busied herself decorating the house in the stillness of the late afternoon. As she placed the nativity on top of the television, her thoughts turned to the first Christmas and the Christ-child who was God's love Gift to the world. How she wished she could share that love with her sister.

Glancing out the window, she saw the mailman stuff another batch of cards in the mailbox. Wrapping her sweater around her, she went outside. All of the envelopes, except one red one, had return addresses. Curious, she turned it over and opened it.

"Please forgive me, Sis," it read. "I apologize for not getting in touch sooner. I hope we can talk." Allison looked at the enclosed photos, and tears sprang to her eyes. Fifteen years was a long time.

When the sisters finally spoke to each other, Allison was surprised to learn that her once-wayward sister was now a believer. "I still have the Bible you gave me when I was six," Beth said. "It's still in the original box, and not only that, I use it."

To Allison's surprise, God had shared His love gift of Jesus with her sister. How awesome is our God when we put our full trust in Him! When we are still in His presence and recognize that He is our sovereign Lord, it allows Him the freedom to work His blessings in our lives.

The more we depend on God, the more
dependable we find he is.

CLIFF RICHARDS

NOTHING IS IMPOSSIBLE

When Jama Hedgecoth was five, she found a hungry cat. Even at that age, Jama loved animals and couldn't stand to see one in need. She begged her mother to let her keep it. When her mother said no, Jama placed her balled-up fists on her hips and said, "Mama, one of these days the Lord is going to give me all the animals I want."

The daughter of traveling evangelists, Jama believed strongly in God. Years later, her faith became reality. Today, Jama is now married with four children and lives on 122 acres of farm county in Georgia, where she began Noah's Ark, a safe haven and rehabilitation center for more than a thousand animals.

When Jama first saw the property, she knew without a doubt that God would give it to her. Her truck driver husband's response was one of disbelief when Jama began packing everything. As boxes piled upwards toward the ceiling, her husband called her minister father and said, "Jama has lost it. She's packing, saying God's going to move us to the property. We don't have a penny. I can't even find my socks."

"I tell you the truth, if you have faith as small as a mustard seed, you can say to this mountain, 'Move from here to there' and it will move. Nothing will be impossible for you."

MATTHEW 17:20

Jama's father merely said, "If God spoke to her, just hang on."

Jama's faith remained strong, even though Noah's Ark passed through troubling waters. Three times, the center was nearly evicted, but God brought one miracle after another. Once when Noah's Ark was near financial ruin, an Atlanta businessman offered to pay off the center's mortgage and build a foster children's home, where twelve children are housed.

A spirit of unconditional love runs through Jama's family. Through her faith in God, Jama has taken in animals that nobody wanted, including wildcats, lions, monkeys, and emus. And she has opened up her heart to foster children as well.

How big is your faith? Sometimes God wants us to step out in our faith—not to prove to Him that we have faith, but to prove to ourselves how much we believe in the power of our God. Are you willing to step out in faith?[47]

To have faith is to believe the task ahead
of us is never as great as the power
behind us.

UNKNOWN

IN JESUS' NAME

Thirty-seven-year-old Joyce Girgenti, a Christian artist, shares her faith by painting the name of Jesus into her inspirational paintings.

In the fall of 1994, Joyce was approached by an organization to raise money for a local boys' club. They wanted her to donate a Christmas card scene. Her first effort, a fireplace scene complete with a Christmas tree and nativity, was turned down. Undaunted, she replaced the scene with another, and it was accepted. Later, she realized why her original scene was rejected— God had other plans.

Joyce had used a photo of her own fireplace to paint the original scene. Working from the top of the canvas, she painted the Christmas tree, the nativity on the mantel, the roaring fire, and the stones that formed the fireplace. As she began to paint the bottom of the fireplace, she turned to her daughter. "Wouldn't it be neat to hide something in the fireplace that refers to Christmas?" she asked.

My purpose is that they may be encouraged in heart and united in love, so that they may have the full riches of complete understanding, in order that they may know the mystery of God, namely, Christ, in whom are hidden all the treasures of wisdom and knowledge.

COLOSSIANS 2:2-3

Before her daughter could answer, Joyce said, "What better than Jesus? He's why we celebrate Christmas." She then arranged the fireplace stones to spell out the name of Jesus.

After her card was originally rejected, Joyce used it to send to clients and friends. One day, Joyce received a call from her friend Mary, who asked, "Is Jesus' name really in your fireplace?"

Standing in front of her fireplace, Joyce took a deep breath. "You're not going to believe this," she said, "but His name is there. I even see a heart-shaped stone."

It's a mystery trying to find Jesus' name so well hidden in Joyce's paintings, but the real mystery is not His name — it is Jesus himself. Only when Jesus is revealed are we able to discern His hidden treasure for us — His gift of salvation.

Salvation is a gift you can ask for.

UNKNOWN

A FLASH PRAYER

The woman stood at the window one winter day watching the wind whipping the pine trees. The cold rain had sneaked in the night before. Early that morning, the woman had struggled to get out of bed as the extreme cold and dampness wreaked havoc on her joints.

> Dear friends, since God so loved us, we also ought to love one another. No one has ever seen God; but if we love one another, God lives in us and his love is made complete in us.
>
> 1 JOHN 4:11-12

At the post office, everyone seemed to feel as she did. No one smiled, and everyone seemed to struggle through the day. She decided then and there to at least change her own outlook. She began to smile—not a forced smile, but a caring smile that radiated the love of Jesus. For some, she whispered a "flash prayer" that their day would be blessed by the Heavenly Father.

Her smiles brought blessings from God in the form of a grandmother who rushed to her side to share a funny story, a man who asked her opinion on which handbag to buy for his wife, and a boy who allowed her take his place in the express lane.

A smile even began a friendship with a young grocery store bagger who had Down syndrome. One winter day with snow clouds slung low across the sky, the young man carried the woman's groceries to her car. Digging in her purse for a tip, she was embarrassed when she found she had nothing to give him.

"I'm sorry," she said, not wanting to disappoint the young man.

A smile as bright as the summer sun spread across his face. "That's okay," he said. Then he wrapped his arms around her. "I love you," he said.

Shivering in the cold, she whispered a "flash prayer" for this very special child of God. "Lord, bless this precious child," she whispered.

When was the last time you whispered a "flash prayer"? Or when was the last time you hugged someone who was different from you? As Christians, we need to be reaching out to all of God's children. It seems that "the least of these" can teach many of us a lesson in humility, but the greatest lesson in humility is found in Jesus Christ.[48]

A smile is a curve that helps to set things straight.

UNKNOWN

THE SECRET GIFT

"When you give to the needy, do not let your left hand know what your right hand is doing so that your giving may be in secret. Then your Father, who sees what is done in secret, will reward you."

MATTHEW 6:3-4

It was the Christmas when Diane's son, Marty, was eight that she witnessed a miracle. Her youngest child, Marty, was filled with excitement even though he had a minor handicap. He was deaf in one ear.

While times had been difficult for her family, Diane knew how much better off she was than Kenny's mom, who lived nearby and struggled daily just to feed and clothe her children.

Several weeks before Christmas, Diane realized that Marty was saving his small allowance for a gift to give Kenny. One day, he strolled into the kitchen and showed her a pocket compass. "I've bought Kenny a present," he said.

Knowing how proud Kenny's mother was, Diane didn't believe she would allow her son to accept a gift if he couldn't give one in return. Marty argued with his mother and finally said, "But what if it was a secret? What if they never found out who gave it?"

Diane finally relented and watched her son walk out the door on Christmas Eve, cross the wet pasture, and slip beneath the electric fence.

He raced up to the door and pressed the doorbell, then ran down the steps and across the yard so he wouldn't be seen. Suddenly, the electric fence loomed in front of him, and it smacked him hard. The shock knocked him to the ground, and he gasped for breath. Slowly, he got up and stumbled home.

Diane treated the blister on Marty's face, then put him to bed. The next day, Kenny came to the front door excitedly talking about his new compass. Amazingly, Marty seemed to hear — with both ears.

Later, the doctor confirmed that Marty somehow regained hearing in his deaf ear. Though the doctor said it may have been the shock from the electric fence, Diane believed that miracles still happen on the night we celebrate our Lord's birth.

What a testimony of love Marty shared with his friend! He wanted to give in secret just as God asks to, and in His faithfulness, Kenny was rewarded for what he did in secret. What good deeds have you done in secret?[49]

He that does good to another does good to himself.

LUCIUS ANNAEUS SENECA

STORMY WEATHER

Elizabeth stared out the window at low-hanging rain clouds. Kissing the top of her newborn's head, she wrapped the blanket around him, wishing her husband was home.

> God did not give us a spirit of timidity, but a spirit of power, of love, and of self-discipline.
>
> 2 TIMOTHY 1:7

That afternoon, the rain started slowly. By nighttime, it had turned into a tap-tapping sound, and Elizabeth realized it was now sleet.

The child opened his slate-blue eyes and cooed. She placed the baby on her lap. As her heart filled with love for this new human being, she felt an inexplicable warmth pass between them. She wondered if perhaps this was the way God felt about His children.

"I'll bet you want something to eat," she said, touching the baby's cheek. She placed him on his side in the playpen. Taking a bottle from the fridge, she put it in a saucepan to warm. When it was ready, she sprinkled the milk on her wrist. Satisfied that it was the right temperature, she gave it to her child.

Later, the sleet turned to freezing rain. Peeking outside, she could see the ice-coated pine trees bowing to their knees. Nervously, she said out loud, "Jim, where are you?"

Just as she started toward the telephone, the lights went out. She found a candle and lit it. As time passed, the house became chilled. She wrapped another blanket around the baby and put a cap on his head, then pulled on her coat.

What if the lights don't come back on soon? What if they don't come on for days? Her mind raced through all the possibilities. Where is my husband? In all this bad weather, has he been in an accident? "Oh, Lord," she whispered, "I'm so afraid."

In the darkness and deepening silence, she heard an inner voice remind her that God is our Refuge and Strength, an ever-present Help in trouble. Within the hour, her husband came home, and not long after, the lights blinked on.

As Christians we know we shouldn't give in to our fears, but we often do. If we cast our doubts and fears at the foot of the cross, Jesus' outstretched arms can more than abundantly fill our needs.

Relinquishment of burdens and fears begins where adoration and worship of God become the occupation of the soul.

FRANCES J. ROBERTS

ACTIVE TRUST

I n her book *Beyond Our Selves*, Catherine Marshall writes about her husband's active trust in God. A popular Presbyterian minister, her husband, Peter Marshall, also served as chaplain of the United States Senate during the late 1940s.

> "Do not let your hearts be troubled, trust in God; trust also in me."
>
> JOHN 14:1

Catherine once said, "I thought that faith was believing this or that specific thing in my mind. Now I know that faith is nothing more or less than actively trusting God." To demonstrate this, she provided an illustration her husband used:

Suppose a child has a broken toy. He brings the toy to his father, saying that he himself has tried to fix it and has failed. He asks his father to do it for him. The father gladly agrees, takes the toy and begins to work. Now obviously the father can do his work most quickly and easily if the child makes no attempt to interfere, simply sits quietly watching, or even goes about other business, with never a doubt that the toy is being successfully mended.

But what do most of God's children do in such a situation? Often we stand by offering a lot of meaningless advice and some rather silly criticism. We even get impatient and try to help, and so get our hands in the Father's way, generally hindering the work.

Finally, in our desperation, we may even grab the toy out of the Father's hands entirely, saying rather bitterly that we hadn't really thought He could fix it anyway . . . that we'd given Him a chance and He had failed us.

Taking the toy from the Father does not show trust. What does exemplify trust is when we put the person or thing we love most into our Father's hands, allowing Him to do as He wills.

Are you placing your loved ones in the generous hands of our Father who knows what is best for His children? Or are you clinging to them, believing only you can protect them? Try putting your trust in a Father who tends His flock like a shepherd, gathering His children in His arms and carrying them close to His heart.[50]

A mighty fortress is our God, a bulwark never failing; our helper he amid the flood of mortal ills prevailing.

MARTIN LUTHER

REFERENCES

Unless otherwise indicated, all Scripture quotations are taken from the Holy Bible, New International Version®. NIV®. Copyright © 1973, 1978, 1984 by International Bible Society. Used by permission of Zondervan Publishing House. All rights reserved.

Scripture quotations marked KJV are taken from the King James Version of the Bible.

Scripture quotations marked NKJV are taken from The New King James Version. Copyright © 1979, 1980, 1982, Thomas Nelson, Inc.

Scripture quotations marked RSV are taken from The Revised Standard Version Bible, copyright © 1946, Old Testament section copyright © 1952 by the Division of Christian Education of the National Council of the Churches of Christ in the United States of America. Used by permission.

Scripture quotations marked AMP are taken from The Amplified Bible. Old Testament copyright © 1965, 1987 by Zondervan Corporation, Grand Rapids, Michigan. New Testament copyright © 1958, 1987 by The Lockman Foundation, La Habra, California. Used by permission.

Scripture quotations marked NASB are taken from the New American Standard Bible. Copyright © The Lockman Foundation 1960, 1962, 1963, 1968, 1971, 1972, 1973, 1975, 1977, 1995. Used by permission.

Verses marked TLB are taken from The Living Bible

ENDNOTES

[1](pp. 10-11) Reader's Digest (October 1991) pp. 59-62.

[2](p. 12) Reader's Digest (March 1991) pp. 128-132.

[3](p. 17) Reader's Digest (December 1992) pp. 101-104.

[4](pp. 24-25) Craig B. Larson, Illustrations for Preaching & Teaching (Grand Rapids, MI: Baker Book House, 1993) p. 106.

[5](pp. 26-27) Ibid., p. 122.

[6](pp. 34-35) Ruth Youngdahl Nelson, God's Song in My Heart (Philadelphia: Fortress Press, 1957) pp. 248-249.

[7](pp. 42-43) Kenneth W. Osbeck, Amazing Grace (Grand Rapids, MI: Kregel Publications, 1990) p. 38.

[8](p. 44) Anne Frank, The Diary of a Young Girl (NY: Doubleday, 1952).

[9](p. 44) Ibid.

[10](pp. 54-55) Reader's Digest (March 1999) p. 117.

[11](pp. 56-57) George Sweeting, Who Said That? (Chicago: Moody Press, 1995).

[12](pp. 64-65) The Misheard Lyrics Website, www.kissthisguy.com.

[13](p. 68) Today in the Word (September 2, 1992).

[14](p. 69) Maya Angelou, Wouldn't Take Nothin' for My Journey Now (NY: Random House, 1993) p. 62.

[15](pp. 72-73) Judy Seymour, "The Freeway Not Taken: Lake Route Worth the Slower Pace," Minneapolis Star

Tribune (May 12, 1997) p. 15A.

[16](p. 74) "Words of Love By Mother Teresa," Education for Democracy, Benjamin R. Barber and Richard M. Battistoni, eds. (Dubuque: Kendall / Hunt Publishing Company, 1993).

[17](pp. 74-75) Ibid.

[18](pp. 80-81) Author unknown.

[19](pp. 82-83) Jean Shepherd, The Endless Streetcar Ride into the Night, and the Tinfoil Noose, in The Riverside Reader, Vol. 1, p. 17.

[20](p. 84) Meryle Secrest, Leonard Bernstein: A Life (Knopf, 1995).

[21](p. 85) Common Ground (January 1990).

[22](p. 87) Linda J. Vogel, Teaching and Learning in Communities of Faith (San Francisco: Jossey-Bass Publishers, 1991) p. 124.

[23](pp. 132-133) Charlie W. Shedd, Brush of an Angel's Wings (Ann Arbor, MI: Servant Publications, 1994).

[24](pp. 152-153) Irene Harrell, Ordinary Days with an Extraordinary God (1971).

[25](p.192) Tony Campolo, "Who Switched the Price Tags?" The Inspirational Study Bible, Max Lucado, ed., (Dallas, TX: Word Publishing, 1995) p. 402.

[26](p.193) Illustrations Unlimited, James W. Hewett, ed. (Wheaton, IL: Tyndale House, 1988) pp. 25-26.

[27](pp. 194-195) A Moment a Day, Mary Beckwith and Kathi Milled, eds. (Ventura, CA: Regal Books, 1988) p. 37.

[28](p. 200) Walter B. Knight, Knight's Master Book of 4,000 Illustrations (Grand Rapids, MI: Eerdmans Publishing Co., 1956) p. 448.

[29](p. 201) Ibid.

[30](pp. 204-205) Paul Lee Tan, Encyclopedia of 7,700 Illustrations (Garland, TX: Bible Communications Inc., 1979) p. 1387.

[31](pp. 206-207) Newsweek (January 22, 1996) p. 14.

[32](p. 212) Webster's New World Dictionary of the American Language (NY: World Publishing Co., 1968) p. 1258.

[33](p. 220) Daily Readings from the Works of Leslie D. Weatherhead, Frank Cumbers, ed. (Nashville, TN: Abingdon Press, 1968) p. 312.

[34](pp. 220-221) The Forbes Scrapbook of Thoughts on the Business of Life (Chicago: Triumph Books, 1992) p. 111.

[35](pp. 224-225) San Luis Obispo Telegram/Tribune (March 9, 1995) p. C8.

[36](p. 234) Helen Simpson, The London Ritz Book of Afternoon Tea (NY: Arbor House, 1986) pp. 6-7.

[37](pp. 238-239) Aubrey Franklin, Teatime by the Tea Ambassador (NY: Frederick Fell Publishers, Inc., 1981) pp. xi-xii.

[38](pp. 242-243) Paul Lee Tan, Encyclopedia of 7700 Illustrations (Garland, TX: Bible Communications Inc., 1979) p. 1477.

[39](pp. 244-245) Aubrey Franklin, Teatime by the Tea Ambassador (NY: Frederick Fell Publishers, Inc., 1981) p. 62.

[40](pp. 246-247) Joni Eareckson Tada, Diamonds in the Dust (Grand Rapids, MI: Zondervan, 1993) February 17 entry.

[41](pp. 252-253) San Francisco Chronicle (February 4, 1996) p. 4.

[42](p. 260) Treasury of Christian Faith, Stanley I. Stuber and Thomas Curtis Clark, eds. (NY: Association Press, 1949) p. 806.

[43](p. 264) W. Phillip Keller, Songs of My Soul, A1 Bryant, ed. (Dallas, TX: Word Publishing, 1989) pp. 100-101,158.

[44](pp. 294-295) Kelly McHugh, "The Upper Room" (January 9, 1999).

[45](pp. 296-297) Patricia D. Brown, 365 Affirmations for Hopeful Living (August 17).

[46](pp. 300-301) Marion Bond West, Look Out Fear, Here Comes Faith! (Ann Arbor, MI: Servant Publications, 1991) pp. 155-158.

[47](pp. 304-305) Nanette Thorsen-Snipes, Georgia Magazine (1999, to be published).

[48](pp. 308-309) Nanette Thorsen-Snipes, Southern Lifestyles (Summer 1996) p. 38.

[49](pp. 310-311) Diane Rayner, The Best Stories from Guideposts (Wheaton, IL: Tyndale House Publishers, 1987) pp. 219-222.

[50](pp. 314-315) Catherine Marshall, Beyond Our Selves (NY: McGraw-Hill, 1961) pp. 87-88.

Additional copies of this book and other titles in the
Quiet Moments with God Devotional series are available
from your local bookstore or online.

Quiet Moments with God
Quiet Moments with God for Mothers
Quiet Moments with God for Couples
Quiet Moments with God for Teachers
Quiet Moments with God for Teens